THE FIRST TIME DAD SURVIVAL GUIDE

A ROADMAP TO THRIVING AS A NEW DAD WITH PRACTICAL ADVICE ON INFANT CARE, CHILD DEVELOPMENT, NAVIGATING FINANCIAL CHALLENGES AND BALANCING WORK & FAMILY

H. S. GRAY

© Copyright 2024 - All rights reserved.

The content contained within this book may not be reproduced, duplicated or transmitted without direct written permission from the author or the publisher.

Under no circumstances will any blame or legal responsibility be held against the publisher, or author, for any damages, reparation, or monetary loss due to the information contained within this book, either directly or indirectly.

Legal Notice:

This book is copyright protected. It is only for personal use. You cannot amend, distribute, sell, use, quote or paraphrase any part, or the content within this book, without the consent of the author or publisher.

Disclaimer Notice:

Please note the information contained within this document is for educational and entertainment purposes only. All effort has been executed to present accurate, up to date, reliable, complete information. No warranties of any kind are declared or implied. Readers acknowledge that the author is not engaged in the rendering of legal, financial, medical or professional advice. The content within this book has been derived from various sources. Please consult a licensed professional before attempting any techniques outlined in this book.

By reading this document, the reader agrees that under no circumstances is the author responsible for any losses, direct or indirect, that are incurred as a result of the use of the information contained within this document, including, but not limited to, errors, omissions, or inaccuracies.

For Cameron,

Your dedication to your craft and devotion to your family is an inspiration.

CONTENTS

Introduction	9
1. DISCOVERING FATHERHOOD	**15**
The Dual Nature of Fatherhood	17
Common Fears New Dads Face	19
Evolving Role in Society	23
Mental and Emotional Preparation	25
Interactive Element: Fatherhood Feelings Journal	27
2. ATTENDING TO BONDING	**31**
The Science of Bonding	32
Touch, Talk, and Play Techniques	34
Skin-to-Skin Contact	38
Integrating Skin-to-Skin Into Daily Life	39
Responding to Baby's Needs	40
Interactive Element: Bonding Activities Checklist	41
3. DIAPERING AND OTHER BASIC CARE	**45**
Diapering Demystified	47
Hygiene and Health Tips	51
What If Baby Is Sick?	53
Feeding Fundamentals	56
Solutions for Typical Newborn Concerns	58
Interactive Element: Baby Care Tracker	61
4. SUPPORTING GROWTH AND DEVELOPMENT	**65**
Decoding Baby's Sleep Patterns	66
Recognizing Emotional Milestones	70
Navigating Developmental Stages	72
Interactive Growth Chart for Your Baby's First Year	78
5. GROWING RELATIONSHIPS AND OVERCOMING CHALLENGES	**81**
Managing Difficult Behaviors	82
Maintaining a Strong Romantic Relationship	86
Relationships With Extended Family	89

Financial and Healthcare Planning	90
Family Relationship Plan Worksheet	94

6. UPHOLDING SAFETY — 101
Childproofing Essentials	102
Creating a Loving Home Atmosphere	107
What Do the Professionals Say?	110
Balancing Personal Development and Fatherhood	111
Self-Care Tips for Dads	112
Interactive Element: Home Safety Checklist	114

7. INSPIRING THROUGH PLAY — 119
Creative Play Ideas	120
Preparation for Early Schooling	123
Instilling Values and Ethics	125
Interactive Element: Parent–Child Play Journal	128

8. DEVELOPING FAMILY HARMONY AND SOCIAL WELL-BEING — 133
Family Physical and Mental Wellness	134
Encouraging Social Skills and Friendships	137
Balancing Work and Fatherhood	139
Interactive Element: Family Wellness Plan	142

9. ENVISIONING THE FUTURE — 147
Celebrating Milestones and Making Memories	148
Adapting to Family's Evolving Needs	152
Leaving a Lasting Legacy	154
Life Lessons From a Father	157
Interactive Element: A Letter to My Future Child (A Template)	158

Conclusion	161
References	167

MEDICAL DISCLAIMER

The content presented in this book is meant for educational and informational purposes exclusively. It should not be considered a replacement for professional medical guidance, diagnosis, or treatment. It is essential to consult your physician or a qualified healthcare professional for any queries related to a medical condition or the well-being of your child. Please do not ignore professional medical advice or postpone seeking it based on information from this book. Relying on the information in this book is entirely at your own discretion.

TRIGGER WARNING

This book may contain content that could be triggering or upsetting to some readers. Topics discussed within this book may include childbirth, postpartum depression, infant loss, and other sensitive subjects related to parenting. Reader discretion is advised. If you find yourself becoming distressed or uncomfortable while reading this book, please seek support from a trusted friend, family member, or mental health professional.

INTRODUCTION

Every day, brave souls like yourself venture into the uncharted territory of fatherhood, a role that has the power to turn your life upside down, inside out, and sideways. It's like being handed a mysterious treasure map without instructions, filled with moments that make you laugh, cry, sigh, and question everything. This book was written as a compass to guide you through the ride of fatherhood. It contains advice, relatable experiences, and hopefully a dose of humor for some levity. This journey will be filled with unexpected twists, heartwarming victories, and the occasional battle against sleep deprivation. But remember, amid the chaos and confusion, you possess the power of love, patience, and earned permission to crack unlimited dad jokes that will make your little ones groan for years to come.

This book is not just a manual; it's a celebration of your extraordinary life, one hilarious and sometimes terrifying step at a time. Get ready to embrace the adventure, learn, grow, and become the legendary dad you were always meant to be!

Let's take a glimpse at some of the things we will explore within these pages—those common struggles that come with the territory of first-time fatherhood:

- **Feeling unprepared for fatherhood:** This is a common experience that many new dads go through. It's that moment when you realize that you have no idea what you're doing and start questioning your abilities as a new parent. The intention of this book is to help you get prepared well before the baby arrives. Is your child already here? No worries; this book is for you, too!
- **Achieving work-life balance:** Being a first-time dad and trying to balance career and family can feel like juggling flaming swords while riding a unicycle in the midst of a hurricane. We will explore viable tips and tricks to make it possible. You've got this!
- **Changing relationship dynamics:** Suddenly, your once peaceful evenings of Netflix and snacks turn into diaper-changing marathons and lullaby sing-offs. And let's not forget the sleep deprivation! But hey, despite the chaos, being a new dad brings a whole new level of love, joy, and adventure to your life. This book acts as a compass guiding you through the newfound life of your ever-evolving relationship.
- **Lack of social support:** Someone handed you a brand new baby, and now there are days when you feel isolated and completely out of your comfort zone. Within these pages, you will find suggestions to help you move through those

uncharted waters when it sometimes feels like you're all alone in this.
- **Coping with mental and emotional health:** When parenthood arrives in your life, it is essential to be prepared for the impact it can have on your mental and emotional state. You will discover practical solutions for brand-new dads like yourself, addressing sleep deprivation and common mental and emotional health issues that often arise.

Now, why did you choose this book? Was it the baby's baffling colic cries that made you question everything? Or perhaps it was the need to bond with your little one and ensure you don't accidentally put the diaper on backward for the seventeenth time? Whether it was a moment of panic, a surge of love, or just an earnest desire to rock this dad thing, I've got you covered. Here's the lowdown on the perks of diving into these pages.

This book serves as your personal guide, simplifying the complexities of parenting into practical, easy-to-follow advice. It provides invaluable shortcuts to mastering essential skills, from the basics of diapering and feeding to the nuances of building emotional bonds that'll make your baby's heart sing. You'll learn how to care for your child and maintain a healthy relationship with your partner (hint: it involves more than just changing diapers together), as well as mastering the art of balancing work and family life without losing your sanity. Best of all? This guide is not a snooze-fest of statistics and baby jargon. It's filled with relatable experiences and tips from seasoned dads that will have you nodding in solidarity and chuckling at the absurdity of it all. This book is your trusty sidekick, your secret weapon in the quest for fatherhood success, and your go-to source for confidence and guidance. Within these chapters, you will be introduced to the D.A.D.S G.U.I.D.E Framework because I like acronyms almost as much as dad jokes!

D—Discovering fatherhood: Unveil the secrets of this new role and the emotional rollercoaster that accompanies it.

A—Attending to bonding: Forge deep emotional connections with your baby.

D—Diapering and care: Become a diaper ninja, a feeding pro, and a hygiene expert.

S—Supporting growth and development: Guide your little human's learning by nurturing their curiosity and wonder as they begin on this crazy little thing we call life.

G—Growing relationships and overcoming challenges: Keep the flame alive with your partner while dealing with parenthood's unpredictable twists and turns.

U—Upholding safety: Create a home that is so safe and loving that it rivals a fluffy cloud of baby joy.

I—Inspiring through play: Make playtime not just fun but a brain-boosting adventure.

D—Developing family harmony and social well-being: Be the maestro conducting a harmonious family symphony while juggling your work, family, and social life.

E—Envisioning the future: Peer into the crystal ball and see the incredible journey of fatherhood while planning your family's financial future.

I know that fatherhood can be terrifying. My job is to remind you that it is also beautiful, rewarding, and filled with surprises and love. From the minute your baby wraps those tiny fingers around one of yours, you are committed to doing whatever it takes to be the best for them. I am just here to offer some help along the way. Are you ready to embark on this heartwarming and sometimes hair-raising adventure? Hold on tight because we're about to start down the path of giggles, poop, and baby breath—and it's going to be one unforgettable ride!

CHAPTER 1
DISCOVERING FATHERHOOD

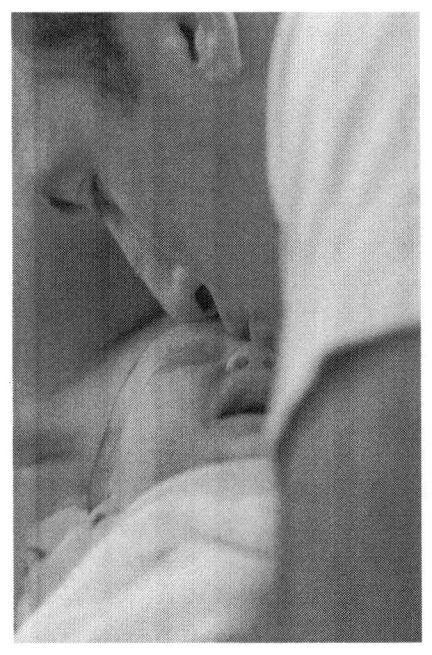

So, you've just welcomed your little bundle of joy into the world, or maybe you're on the cusp of it. Either way, get ready for a whirlwind of emotions, challenges, and unforgettable moments.

Let's kick things off with a little brain teaser: How does the birth of a child redefine a man's identity? No, seriously, take a moment to ponder that. It's not just a philosophical question; it's the real deal. Becoming a dad is like hitting the "reset" button on your existence. Suddenly, you're not just you anymore. You are a dad. And that changes everything.

Now, I won't sugarcoat it. Nope, along with the overwhelming joy comes a healthy dose of fear and doubt. Are you up to the task? Can you handle the responsibility of shaping another human being? Spoiler alert: Yes, you can. But it's okay to feel a little shaky at first. We're all in the same leaky boat here.

In this chapter, we're beginning with the first stage of the D.A.D.S. G.U.I.D.E. Framework. We'll explore the highs and lows of fatherhood, from the heart-melting moments of bonding with your baby to the gut-wrenching anxiety of wondering if you're doing it all wrong. And guess what? That is totally normal. Every dad goes through it. So, consider this your guide in embracing the chaos and finding your footing in this new role.

Along with the challenges come some pretty amazing perks. Like watching your mini-me take their first wobbly steps or hearing their infectious giggle for the first time. Trust me, those moments make all the sleepless nights and spit-up stains totally worth it.

So, grab your diaper bag and hold on tight because fatherhood is one unforgettable ride. Welcome to the club, Dad.

THE DUAL NATURE OF FATHERHOOD

Alright, let's dive into the whirlwind of emotions, which is the dual nature of fatherhood. Picture this: You're on cloud nine, bursting with pride and joy as you anticipate the arrival of your little bundle of potential world changer. But hold onto your hat because right alongside that excitement, there's a sneaky undercurrent of anxiety about what this new chapter will mean for you.

Most soon-to-be dads are terrified! They—much like you—realize they are soon going to be responsible not just for keeping a new child alive but for molding them into a decent member of society. The weight of that is heavy, and it is natural to feel uneasy.

Let's hear what some seasoned dads have to say. Real talk from real dads might just ease some of those jitters or, at the very least, show you that you're not alone in this adventure.

Take Ian, for example. He expected this thunderbolt moment when he first held his child, but it didn't happen. He felt awkward, and there was no immediate connection. He watched as his wife sobbed and commented to everyone about the strong bond she felt. Ian? He said this baby felt like a stranger. And you know what? That's okay. The journey to unconditional love isn't always a sprint; sometimes, it's a marathon. Over time, as this sweet boy learned to hold his daddy's finger and smile at him, Ian's heart and bond grew.

Then there's Mike, feeling like a bit of a third wheel in those early days. His new daughter came home, and he melted into the background. Visitors came for days bringing gifts for the baby and his wife, barely acknowledging him in the room. There were questions about how the baby was doing and how his wife was doing, but never a mention of how he was holding up. His wife was the MVP of baby feeding and bonding with their daughter, but he felt useless and invisible. After a bit, he confided in his wife how he was feeling, and they made a plan to include Mike more. These growing pains are all normal.

And Eric? He had grand plans to be the ultimate 50-50 partner in baby duty, but sometimes life gets messy. Two weeks before his son arrived, he broke his leg, which put him out of commission. He started to feel more of a burden than a help. He had to realize that there are just going to be times when you have to do the best you can to support your partner. Your best is good enough.

Nate? He admits to being downright terrified of babies at first. He was 35 years old and had never even held one. If he was being honest, they creeped him out. Everyone told him that he would feel differently about his own child, and guess what? He did not. When he looked at his premature son, he shook with fear. He refused to hold him, convinced he would hurt him. It took a week for his partner to convince him that he needed to bond with his son, and he gently laid their son on his chest. The warmth of his sweet boy made him fall instantly in love, and he knew, at that moment, that he would do anything to protect him for life.

Hunter, on the other hand, feels the weight of the world on his shoulders, wishing he could protect his child from every bump and bruise that life throws their way. His wife isn't even due for another four weeks, and the anxiety and worry keep him awake at night. Every horrible scenario imaginable plays out in his head. The third time his wife caught him pacing the house at 3:00 a.m., she suggested he talk to someone. He found an online support group for dads, and they were honest in telling him he wouldn't be able to protect his child from everything. At this stage, he needs to focus on what he can control: keeping his wife and himself healthy, providing the necessities for his child, and enjoying all the great moments.

COMMON FEARS NEW DADS FACE

Prepare yourself as we delve into the realm of common fears that may be causing you sleepless nights. Rest assured, I am here to provide you with guidance on how to address each fear effectively:

Fear #1: "Will I do everything right?"

- Try to relax. No one expects perfection from you. Parenting is a journey of continuous learning. Have confidence in yourself, embrace lessons from mistakes, and enjoy the experience.

Fear #2: "I fear not being able to properly provide for my family once the baby is here."

- This fear is common. However, it is essential to remember that provision extends beyond monetary means. Love, support, and presence hold immeasurable value as well. You are capable and equipped to navigate this!

Fear #3: "I'm scared that everything we do will now be centered around babies."

- Parenthood adds some baby-shaped spice to your life, sure, but it doesn't mean your identity evaporates. Embrace the changes while still nurturing your interests and hobbies.

Fear #4: "I guess my biggest concern is that having a baby will force me to grow up."

- Ah, the perpetual conflict between adulthood and the inner child. While adjustments to your schedule may be necessary, it doesn't signify the end of enjoyment.

Fear #5: "Lack of sleep because I need my sleep."

- Sleep deprivation poses a significant challenge in parenthood. However, rest assured that you will establish a routine with coffee as your reliable companion.

Fear #6: "Something will be wrong with my baby."

- It is natural to worry, but remember, most of the time, babies are just fine. There is no need to worry unless an issue presents itself. Stay informed, trust your instincts, and lean on your support system when needed.

Fear #7: "All the clutter that will be all around the house."

- Get ready for the invasion of baby gear! Embrace the chaos, but don't hesitate to declutter when things get out of hand. A small amount of organization can have a significant impact.

Fear #8: "Failing as a father."

- Your awareness is your greatest asset. Love, respect, and being there for your little one will take you far.

Fear #9: "Not being able to 'soothe' my baby when it cries."

- It's a trial-and-error process. Experiment with different techniques, from rocking to singing to funny faces. Your baby might surprise you with what works like magic.

Practical Advice to Overcome Them

Before we explore practical solutions to those problems that keep you awake at night, I want to validate your feelings. As men, you are often told that your emotions don't matter or that you should suck it up and get your crap together. Nothing could be further from the truth. Talking about these issues now is healthy. This gives you the opportunity to deal with your fears in a constructive way and be the best dad you can be. Great job!

Lack of Sleep

Yeah, sleep deprivation is no joke. But here's what you have to remember—you're tougher than you think. Sleep in short bursts when you can, and don't be afraid to enlist some help from your partner or family. And hey, coffee is your best friend now. Embrace it. Be mindful that this isn't forever.

Not Being Able to Soothe Baby

Guess what? Babies can be like puzzles sometimes. But don't sweat it if you can't crack the code right away. Experiment with different soothing techniques. All babies are different, and how they like to be soothed can change daily. Try rocking, singing, or swaddling until you find what works for your little bundle of joy. And remember, it's okay to ask for help if you need it.

Not Being a Good Dad

Newsflash: Nobody is born an expert in this dad stuff. Being a good dad is about showing up, being present, and loving your child with all your heart. That is the foundation. You'll make mistakes, every parent does, but as long as you're doing your best, you're already light years ahead.

Dealing With Added Baby Gear Around the House

All the added baby gear is truly chaos, isn't it? Start by organizing things in a way that makes sense to you. And don't be afraid to streamline. You don't need every gadget on the market. Less clutter, less stress. It is important to pack it away as baby outgrows it as well. No longer need it? Away it goes!

The Baby Won't Be Healthy

This one hits close to home for all of us. But here's the reality check: Worrying won't change a thing. Focus on what you can control—like keeping up with those doctor appointments and making sure your little one gets plenty of love and care.

I Want to Still Have Fun and Be Youthful

Who says being a dad means you have to give up your inner child? Sure, responsibilities have shifted, but that doesn't mean you can't still have fun. Embrace your silly side; build pillow forts, have dance parties, and make funny faces. Your kids will love it, and you'll feel like a kid again.

Not Being Able to Do Anything Right

What exactly is right, and who has this master guide? What's right for you and your baby may not be right for another family. You're doing better than you think. Cut yourself some slack. Fatherhood is no joke, and it takes years, not days, to master. Just when we think we have parenting figured out, our babies turn into teens, and we have no idea what we are doing all over again. Celebrate the wins—big and small—and remember that every stumble is just another step toward mastering this dad thing.

Being Able to Provide

It's natural to worry about providing for your family. Remember that being a provider goes beyond just bringing home the bacon. It's about being there for your loved ones, supporting them however you can, and creating a loving, nurturing environment. And hey, financial stability is important, but so is emotional support and quality time. You've got more to offer than you realize.

Losing Connection With My Partner

Parenthood is a wild ride, but don't forget about your partner in crime. You can avoid distance by making time for each other. With a new baby, this can look different now. It may be a picnic on the living room floor or a romantic breakfast in bed. Communicate openly, show appreciation, and don't be afraid to ask for help when you need it. You're a team, remember?

EVOLVING ROLE IN SOCIETY

Let's discuss the evolution of dads' roles in society. We're not just talking about them being the traditional breadwinners anymore. Nope, the modern-day father comes in all shapes and sizes, and it is about time we embrace that.

Back in the day, dads were often seen as the stoic figures bringing home the only income while Mom handled everything else on the home front. But oh, how times have changed! Today, dads are breaking free from those old stereotypes and stepping into a variety of roles.

Whether you're single or married, working outside the home or staying in to wrangle the little ones, gay or straight, an adoptive or step-parent, you name it—there's no one-size-fits-all definition of fatherhood anymore. And you know what? That's pretty awesome.

Psychological research has shown that a father's involvement and affection in their kids' lives are key players in their social and emotional development (*The Daddy Factor*, n.d.). So, whether you're changing diapers, coaching soccer practice, or helping with homework, every bit of love and support you give makes a difference.

A Cultural Perspective

First stop: Japan. Over there, fatherhood is all about being the rock-solid provider. Dads are expected to work hard and provide, but they also take on a pretty active role in their kids' lives. Think coaching sports teams and attending school events; they're all in.

Next up, we're jetting over to Italy. Italian dads are all about family, and I mean *all* about it. They're the kings of quality time, whether it's sharing a meal together or taking leisurely strolls through the piazza with their bambinos in tow. They take a very active role in the upbringing of their children.

Now, let's head to Nigeria. In many Nigerian cultures, fatherhood is a deeply respected role. Dads are seen as wise mentors, proudly passing down traditions and values to their children. Plus, they're known for their storytelling skills, bedtime tales with a side of life lessons.

Last but not least, let's swing by Sweden. Those Scandinavian dads are all about equality. Yep, you heard me right. They're not just about providing. Swedish fathers often take parental leave to spend quality time with their children, showing that being a dad is about more than just work.

MENTAL AND EMOTIONAL PREPARATION

First, let's discuss preparing yourself for the task at hand. This unique endeavor requires you to be mentally and emotionally prepared for the challenges ahead. Here are a few strategies to help you get there:

- **Mindfulness:** Taking a few deep breaths and being present in the moment can work wonders. Mindfulness can be your secret weapon when you're knee-deep in dirty diapers and sleepless nights. Mindfulness is about paying attention to your thoughts, feelings, and sensations without judgment. It's about being aware of what's happening in the present moment, whether you're taking a walk or cuddling your baby. When you practice mindfulness, you train your brain to focus, reduce stress, and improve your overall well-being.
- **Seek support:** I know it might feel like it, but you're not in this alone. Reach out to other dads who've been there and done that. They'll have some pearls of wisdom to share, and it's nice to know you're not the only one navigating this journey.
- **Educate yourself:** Knowledge is power. Dive into some parenting resources, whether it's books, websites, or apps. Understanding what to expect can help ease any anxieties you might have.

- **Talk about it:** Don't bottle up those feelings. Whether you're excited, scared, or somewhere in between, talk it out with your partner, friends, or even a therapist if you need to. Trust me; it's okay not to have it all figured out.
- **Self-care:** Take care of yourself. Get enough sleep (while you still can), eat well, and carve out some time for activities you enjoy. A happy dad makes for a happy family.
- **Stay flexible:** Let's face it, parenthood is unpredictable. Plans will go out the window, tantrums will happen, and sleep will become a distant memory. Roll with the punches, and remember that it's all part of the adventure.
- **Make the big announcement:** Once you are ready, share the news with friends and family. Plan a party or make it intimate with just a few close people. Celebrate this amazing time.
- **Be present:** Attend all medical appointments and ultrasound sessions with your partner. This will also ease any anxiety and worry you have about the health of your baby.
- **Learn:** Understand the stages of pregnancy, the child's development, and the changes your partner will experience. The more you learn about what your partner's body is undergoing, the better you can empathize.
- **Take classes:** Take prenatal classes and parenting courses with your partner. The more you know, the better prepared you will feel.
- **Get ready:** Nobody likes to feel like they are heading into something unprepared. Discuss the birth plan with your partner and collaborate on the arrangements together. Know the details and feel like you are ready to go.

- **Get the details:** If there is anything you are unsure of, ask. Ask your healthcare provider any questions you have about the baby's development or the birthing process.
- **Hear your partner out:** Actively listen to your partner's fears and concerns, showing sensitivity to their needs and emotions and offering reassurance and encouragement.
- **Provide assistance:** Pitch in some extra help around the house. Help with household chores and responsibilities to ease your partner's load.
- **What to call baby:** This is a big decision. Discuss and decide on the baby's name.
- **Baby-proof the house:** Choose the necessities and set up the nursery. Purchase the items you will need once the baby arrives.
- **Bond:** Engage in activities that promote bonding with the baby, such as talking, reading, or singing to the baby bump.

Mental and emotional readiness is the key to surviving and thriving in the unpredictable world of fatherhood. So take a deep breath, embrace the chaos, and enjoy.

INTERACTIVE ELEMENT: FATHERHOOD FEELINGS JOURNAL

I would like you to jot down your initial feelings about becoming a dad. What are your biggest fears? What are your hopes and dreams for this new chapter in your life? Go ahead, spill it all out. We'll revisit this later down the road and see how far you've come.

Feel free to pour your heart out, Dad! This journal is for your eyes only, a safe space to explore your emotions as you embark on this incredible journey called fatherhood.

Date: _____

Initial Feelings:

Biggest Fears:

Hopes and Dreams:

In this chapter, we've tackled everything from impending fatherhood to the overwhelming joy of holding your newborn for the first time. We've covered the highs, the lows, and all the messy bits in between.

Remember, it's okay to feel a little lost at times. None of us come into this world as parenting experts. It's a journey of learning, adapting, and growing alongside your little one.

Now, it's time to put all these ideas into action. Dive headfirst into diaper duty, embrace those sleepless nights (as much as one can), and soak in every precious moment with your bundle of joy.

As you start to embrace your role as a dad, the next step is forging a deep, loving bond with your baby. In the next chapter, we'll explore the heart of father-child relationships, from the first touch to building a lifelong connection. Get ready to dive even deeper into the wonderful world of fatherhood.

CHAPTER 2
ATTENDING TO BONDING

So, you've begun this whirlwind adventure called fatherhood. Prepare yourself as we delve deeply into the second stage of the D.A.D.S. G.U.I.D.E. Framework—one of the most enchanting aspects of the journey: forming a bond with your newborn.

But first, let me hit you with a little nugget of dad wisdom: Did you know that babies can recognize their father's voice from as early as 18 weeks in the womb (Shu, 2023)? Your mini-me has been eavesdropping on your conversations from the cozy confines of the womb like a tiny spy-in-training. So, how does this shape the bonding process from day one? That is what we're here to unpack.

In this chapter, I'm going to equip you with the tools and techniques to forge an unbreakable connection with your little sidekick. We're talking touch, talk, play, and yes, even a bit of skin-to-skin action.

By the time we're done here, you'll be dishing out dad jokes with the best of them while effortlessly responding to your baby's every coo and cry like a seasoned professional. So, grab your diaper bag, adjust your dad hat, and let's dive into the wonderful world of bonding.

THE SCIENCE OF BONDING

Bonding is not just about those adorable cuddle sessions, although those are pretty awesome, too. There's some solid science behind why bonding with your baby early on is crucial.

Biological benefits:

- **Promotes infant health and development:** Your loving attention during those first precious moments after birth isn't just heartwarming; it's actually boosting your baby's brainpower. Studies show that early bonding reduces

cognitive delays, helps preterm infants gain weight, and even improves breastfeeding rates. So, those skin-to-skin cuddles aren't just for show—they're like brain-building workouts for your little one (Winston & Chicot, 2016).
- **Stimulates hormonal responses:** Did you know that when you snuggle up with your baby, your body releases a cocktail of feel-good hormones? Endorphins and oxytocin flood your system, making you feel all warm and fuzzy inside. Plus, it's a stress-buster for both of you (Ben-Joseph, 2018). So, go ahead and soak up those baby snuggles—they're good for your health!

Emotional benefits:

- **Supports emotional and social development:** Your role in your baby's life goes beyond just changing diapers and burping. Your consistent love and care set the stage for a strong emotional connection. This isn't just about now; it's about laying the groundwork for a lasting bond that'll shape your child's emotional well-being.
- **Strengthens father-child relationship:** That magical skin-to-skin contact isn't just a bonding moment; it's like hitting the fast-forward button on your relationship with your baby. Holding your little one close in those crucial first hours helps lower their stress levels and promotes calm behavior. Plus, it's a confidence booster for you, knowing you're making a real difference in your baby's life from the get-go.
- **Boosts father's confidence and self-esteem:** Nothing builds it quite like seeing your baby respond positively to your care. Those snuggles and smiles are all little

affirmations that you're doing a great job, Dad. Soak it in; you've earned it.
- **Promotes resilience in children:** Here's a mind-blowing fact: Your bond with your baby now can actually shape their future resilience to stress. Yep, you heard that right. By being there for them, you're laying the groundwork for a strong, resilient child who can take on whatever life throws their way (Winston & Chicot, 2016).
- **Encourages active father involvement:** Your active involvement isn't just nice to have; it's crucial for your child's healthy development. Those early experiences shape their brains, their social skills, and even their ability to handle stress down the road.

Remember, bonding isn't a one-time thing; it's a journey. So cherish those moments, embrace the challenges, and know that every little cuddle and soothing word is shaping your baby's world in ways you can't even imagine.

TOUCH, TALK, AND PLAY TECHNIQUES

Let's discuss touch, talk, and play techniques that will strengthen your relationship with your baby and make you feel like the superhero parent you are destined to be.

- **Master the five S's:** Alright, buckle up for the ultimate calming hack—the five S's. These are your secret weapons to soothe your baby. Some babies might need all five, while others just need a couple to hit the chill button. Once you've got these down, you'll be the calming king of the neighborhood. And hey, did you know dads often excel at this? Yep, you're about to become a baby-calm whisperer. We're talking about:

- **Swaddling:** Swaddling is like baby burrito-making 101! It's all about snugly wrapping your baby in a cozy blanket to mimic the feeling of being in the womb. This gentle, secure wrapping helps soothe babies by preventing their startle reflexes and promoting better sleep. It's like giving them a warm hug from the outside! To swaddle, lay a blanket flat, fold down one corner, and place your baby with their head above the folded corner. Then, gently wrap one side of the blanket snugly across their body and tuck it under their back. Next, fold up the bottom corner over their feet, leaving room for their hips to move. Finally, wrap the other side of the blanket across their body and tuck it in securely.
- **Side or stomach positioning:** Side or stomach positioning refers to placing your baby on their side or stomach while they are awake and under supervision. The change in position from lying on their back may offer a calming sensation for some babies. It can provide a different perspective and help distract them from any discomfort they may be feeling.
- **Shushing:** It's all about creating a soothing white noise sound similar to what babies hear in the womb. This gentle "shh" sound can work wonders in calming your little one down when they're feeling fussy or overwhelmed. So, how does it work? Well, think about it like this: Your baby spent nine months in the cozy confines of the womb, where they were surrounded by all sorts of comforting sounds, including the whooshing of blood flow and mom's heartbeat. Shushing mimics those familiar sounds, triggering a sense of security

and calmness in your baby's brain. Try making a rhythmic "shh" sound close to your baby's ear but not too loud to shush effectively. You want it to be just loud enough to drown out other noises and distractions. You can use your mouth or even a white noise machine to create a soothing sound.

- **Swinging:** Swinging is like giving your baby a gentle ride on the relaxation express! It's one of those age-old tricks that seem to work like a charm when it comes to soothing fussy little ones. Your baby spent months floating around in the womb, gently rocked by mom's movements. Swinging mimics that soothing sensation, reminding your baby of the cozy environment they were used to before making their grand entrance into the world. So, whether you're gently swaying in your arms or using a baby swing, swinging is a tried-and-true method for soothing your little one.
- **Sucking**: One of those instinctual behaviors that babies are born with, and it's a powerhouse when it comes to soothing. Babies are born with a strong sucking reflex that kicks in when they're hungry or seeking comfort. Sucking on a pacifier, thumb, or even your finger provides a sense of security and familiarity for your little one, reminding them of the comforting feeling of breastfeeding.
- **Playtime galore:** It's time to unleash your inner kid! Rough and tumble play is the way to go. Think tickle fights and maybe even a little wrestling (gently, of course). It's not just fun for them; it is a bonding bonfire for you both, fueled by oxytocin, dopamine, and all the good stuff. So, let loose and get playing!

- **Embrace diaper duty:** Yep, you heard me right. Diaper duty isn't just about keeping things clean; it's a bonding bonanza. So, roll up those sleeves and dive in. Your baby will thank you for it (maybe not with words, but definitely with smiles).

Using these techniques can help you become a master at calming your baby, building your confidence, and strengthening your bond.

Jason's Story

When my partner was pregnant, I stressed about many things. Will I have the crib together in time, will I baby proof well enough, will our baby be healthy. The one thing I never worried about was bonding.

Two days after we brought our son home, I realized this was an issue. I soon discovered that society paints a very different picture of parenthood. It isn't realistic. In no television show, movie, or social media profile did I ever see a new father who felt completely secure on the outside. I never imagined how it would feel, watching my partner being the only source of food and the biggest source of comfort, while I walked around, having no idea what to do.

I felt helpless because I couldn't get him to stop crying. Then, my partner held him, and he stopped immediately. I had to figure out my own way. What worked was just doing nothing with my son. I had to stop thinking there was going to be this beautiful moment filled with rainbows. I started sitting in the rocking chair on the front porch with him. I stopped trying to force everything. I slowed it all down and just tried to be present in the moment.

SKIN-TO-SKIN CONTACT

So, picture this: you, shirt off, baby nestled against your bare chest. It's like you're a human hot water bottle but with way more love and cuddles. Here's why this magical skin-to-skin thing is so darn awesome (Steen, 2023).

First, it's relaxing for both of you. Yep, that's right; it calms you down just as much as it calms your mini-me. Say farewell to stress and welcome Zen vibes.

Skin-to-skin time helps regulate your baby's heart rate and breathing, making them feel cozy and secure in this big old world outside the womb. Plus, it kickstarts their digestion and makes them more interested in chowing down.

Oh, and did I mention the temperature control? Forget fancy gadgets; your body's got it covered. Your warmth helps keep your little one just the right amount of toasty.

Now, here's where it gets even cooler. Your skin is like a protector, keeping your baby safe from nasty bugs. Yep, your friendly bacteria transfer during skin-to-skin time, giving your wee one an immune system boost.

And hey, if your little sidekick ends up in the neonatal unit for a bit, skin-to-skin contact is a huge benefit. It boosts oxygen levels, reduces stress (for both of you), and even helps with their growth spurt. Plus, it might just shorten their stay in the hospital.

A study discovered that engaging in skin-to-skin contact assists fathers in connecting and bonding with their babies in a neonatal setting, leading to a beneficial effect on fathers' confidence and self-esteem. One father expressed (Steen, 2023):

After enduring all the stress, I find solace in the calming effect of skin-to-skin contact. As I sit and unwind, embracing my child becomes a source of joy and relaxation for both of us. It's a moment to escape the constant demands and worries, allowing us to unwind and find peace. (p.7)

So there you have it, Dad. Skin-to-skin contact isn't just a feel-good moment; it's like giving your baby a superpower boost while keeping you both feeling calm. So go ahead, strip off that shirt, and get ready for some serious bonding time.

INTEGRATING SKIN-TO-SKIN INTO DAILY LIFE

I've got some practical tips to weave that precious skin-to-skin time seamlessly into your daily routine. Let's get started:

- **Schedule dedicated time:** Carve out 10 or 15 minutes daily for quality skin-to-skin contact. It's like a mini-vacation from the chaos of the world, where you and your baby can just be together in the moment.
- **Create a calm environment:** Set the mood for relaxation. Cue up some soothing tunes, sip on some tea, and ensure you have all the essentials within arm's reach. A hydrated dad is a happy dad!
- **Be awake and alert:** Safety first. Make sure you're fully conscious during the skin-to-skin time. If exhaustion hits hard, laying your little one down in their crib and catching some Z's is okay. We've all been there.

- **Baby wearing:** Strap that bundle of joy to your chest and go about your day. Babywearing keeps your little nugget close while giving you the freedom to conquer your to-do list. Plus, it's a bonding bonanza!
- **Practice soothing:** When your baby needs some TLC, embrace the power of touch. Skin-to-skin snuggles, gentle shushing, sweet lullabies, and soothing eye contact work wonders for both of you.

RESPONDING TO BABY'S NEEDS

Alright, new dad, let's talk baby cues. You know, those little signs your baby throws your way that can seem like a secret code at first, but trust me, you'll crack it. Here's a rundown of some baby language and what they might mean:

- **Arching their back:** This could be anything from gas to reflux to just plain old frustration. Babies, they're like tiny detectives with their own mystery cases. First, check the diaper situation. If that is all clear, try some gentle belly rubs or hold your baby upright to ease gas. And hey, if all else fails, a little cuddle never hurts.
- **Constant kicking:** If your little one seems more playful than Messi on the field, it's probably playtime! Babies love to move and groove, and those kicks might just be their way of saying, "Let's play!"
- **Grabbing their ears:** Teething might be the culprit here, especially when those pesky molars decide to make an appearance. It's like having a tiny construction site in their gums. Keep an eye out for an elevated temperature, which could indicate an ear infection. Don't hesitate to reach out to your pediatrician.

- **Clenched fists:** According to the CDC, those little fists could signal that it's chow time (Guntreddi, 2017). It's time to break out the milk bar!
- **Scrunched-up knees:** This fetal position might not be as comfy for them as it looks. It could mean they're dealing with some tummy discomfort, whether it's gas, a poo-pocalypse, or constipation city.
- **Arm jerks:** No need to call the Ghostbusters when your baby suddenly throws their arms out like they're re-enacting an action movie scene. It's just the Moro reflex, their built-in alarm system for startling sounds or sudden movements (Guntreddi, 2017).

Keep your baby cue decoder ring handy, and remember, you've got this parenting thing in the bag. Just roll with the punches (or kicks, in this case) and enjoy the ride!

INTERACTIVE ELEMENT: BONDING ACTIVITIES CHECKLIST

Here's a handy bonding activities checklist to keep track of your father-baby adventures:

- **Skin-to-skin time:** It's not just for moms! Get that shirt off and snuggle up with your baby. It's an instant bonding booster.
- **Babywearing adventures:** Strap on that baby carrier and hit the town or just pace around the house. Your baby will love the closeness.

- **Storytime serenades:** Pick out some colorful board books and read them aloud to your baby. They might not understand the words yet, but they'll love the sound of your voice.
- **Sing-along sessions:** You don't need to be the next American Idol; just belt out some tunes while you're changing diapers or giving baths. Bonus points if you make up silly songs on the spot.
- **Baby massage:** Gently massage your baby with some baby-safe oil. It's not only relaxing for them but also a great way to bond through touch.
- **Playtime palooza:** Get down on the floor and play with your baby. Whether it's peek-a-boo, gentle tickles, or making funny faces, engage in their world of wonder.
- **Outdoor expeditions:** Take your baby for a stroll in the park or just around the block. Fresh air does wonders for both of you, and it's a great opportunity to chat about the wonders of nature (even if your baby can't respond yet).
- **Dance parties:** Put on some tunes and bust a move with your baby in your arms. They might not be able to dance yet, but they'll enjoy the rhythm and movement.
- **Bedtime rituals:** Establish a soothing bedtime routine with your baby, whether it's a warm bath followed by a lullaby or simply some cuddle time before tucking them in.

Personal Notes

Use this space to jot down your thoughts and feelings during these bonding moments. It's a great way to reflect on your experiences and see how your bond with your baby grows over time.

You've made it through the chapter on building that unbreakable bond with your bundle of joy. Pat yourself on the back because you're already doing a fantastic job. From those tender cuddles to mastering the art of soothing cries, you've been putting in the work, and it's paying off.

Remember, bonding with your baby is a journey, not a race. So, keep those snuggles coming, engage in plenty of skin-to-skin time, and don't be afraid to talk, sing, or even dance with your little one. These simple actions lay the foundation for a strong and lasting connection that will continue to grow over time.

But hey, it's not all mushy feelings and heartwarming moments. Next up, we're jumping into the world of diapering and other basic care. Get ready to tackle those dirty diapers like a professional and master the art of keeping your baby clean, comfortable, and content.

In the next chapter, I'll equip you with the essential skills every new dad needs to navigate infant care with confidence.

CHAPTER 3
DIAPERING AND OTHER BASIC CARE

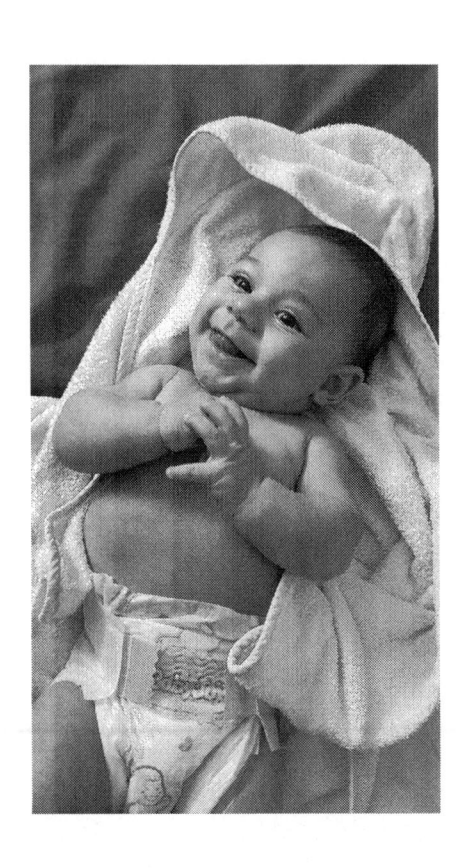

Can the way you diaper and feed your baby impact its long-term health and development? Let's explore the possibilities.

Here, we are at the third stage of the D.A.D.S. G.U.I.D.E. Framework. Now, I know what you're thinking—diapers, hygiene, and basic care might not sound like the most thrilling topics on the planet. Please bear with me because they are essential.

Think about it: You're about to start a life where every little thing you do has an impact on your little one's well-being. From the way you soothe them to the way you change their diapers, it all matters. And trust me, once you get the hang of it, you'll find joy in the simple act of caring for your newborn.

In this chapter, we're exploring diapering and other essential care tasks. We'll cover everything from choosing the right diaper size to mastering the art of the quick-change, all while maintaining your sanity. Plus, we'll touch on hygiene practices that will keep your baby healthy and happy.

But it's not just about the mechanics of diapering and bathing. We're also going to chat about feeding options and schedules because, let's face it, a well-fed baby is a happy baby. Whether you're bottle-feeding or mastering the art of breastfeeding support for your partner, I've got you covered.

And let's not forget about creating a safe and nurturing environment for your little one to thrive in. We'll explore how to baby-proof your home and set up a cozy space where your baby can play, sleep, and grow.

By the end of this chapter, you'll be a diaper-changing, feeding-scheduling, baby-loving machine. Let's dive in and become the powerhouses our little ones need us to be.

DIAPERING DEMYSTIFIED

Alright, Dad, let's tackle diapering like seasoned professionals!

Prep time:

1. Lay down a disposable liner or towel on your diaper-changing surface. This can save you valuable time in the event of a mess.
2. If you're planning to use diaper cream, get it ready now.
3. Gather your gear. Be prepared with everything you need before taking the diaper off. Have a clean diaper, wipes, diaper cream, a bag for any messy clothes, and spare outfits because accidents happen!

Clean-up operation:

1. Lay your little one down on the changing surface and undo the diaper.
2. If you are changing a boy, always keep a wipe over their groin area to avoid surprise streams of urine.
3. Grab those wipes and clean the diaper area gently. Remember, always wipe from front to back to avoid moving fecal matter into unwanted places and causing infection.
4. Bag up any soiled clothing pronto and keep them well away from anything you don't want to get messy.
5. Always keep one hand on the baby for safety reasons. They can move around quicker than you might think.

Bin the junk:

1. Toss used wipes into the old diaper, fold it up and use the sticky tabs to seal it.
2. Move it to the side or to the floor, ready for disposal once baby is changed.

Fresh start:

1. Slide a fresh diaper under your baby.
2. If you're using diaper cream, dab it on gently with a tissue or a clean finger.
3. Fasten up that diaper securely and redress your wee one.
4. It is time to give your little one's hands a wash. Use a clean baby wipe, and be sure to get in between those fingers.
5. Move your baby to a safe and supervised spot.

Tidy up time:

1. Take this time to dispose of the used diaper.
2. Any visible mess? Wipe down the changing table.
3. Time to disinfect! Use a disinfectant spray or wipe suitable for your changing surface, and be sure to follow the instructions.
4. Preparing the area for the next diaper change is also a great idea. It can be a lifesaver for those unexpected, hurried messes.

Clean hands club:

1. Last but not least, give those hands of yours a thorough scrub with soap and water.

There you have it! Diaper duty demystified, conquered, and ready for your next mission.

Diaper Variations

So, let's break it down—we've got the classics, the eco-friendly warriors, and everything in between.

- **Disposable diapers:** These babies are like the trusty steed of the diaper world. Super absorbent? Check. Leak-proof? Double check. With their adhesive tabs and elastic leg cuffs, they're your go-to for quick changes, whether you're at home or on the run. They have convenience written all over them.
- **Cloth diapers:** Guess who's making a comeback? Cloth diapers! Made from soft, breathable fabrics like cotton and bamboo, they keep your little one cozy while also saving the planet. Erase those images of white cloth and safety pins. With all the cute designs and Velcro closures, you can diaper your baby in style.
- **Biodegradable diapers:** If you're all about that green life, biodegradable diapers might be for you. Made from plant-based materials, these diapers break down naturally over time, reducing their impact on the environment. They're gentle on your baby's skin and Mother Earth!

Choosing the right diaper is not just about picking the fanciest-looking one off the shelf. There are a few things to consider:

- **Size:** Make sure you're picking the right size diaper for your little bundle of joy. You don't want anything too snug

or too loose. If it's too loose, you are asking for trouble with leaks!
- **Absorbency:** If your baby's a heavy wetter or a champion sleeper, you'll want something that can handle those marathon diaper sessions without any leaks or accidents.
- **Comfort:** Look for diapers crafted from gentle, breathable materials that won't cause irritation to your baby's sensitive skin. After all, a diaper rash equals a cranky baby.
- **Cost:** Diapers can be a hefty expense, so it's worth shopping around for the best deals and discounts. Bulk buying and subscription services can be your best friend in this department.

Lastly, trust your instincts. You know your baby better than anyone else, so if something doesn't feel right, don't be afraid to switch things up until you find the perfect fit.

Here are some statistics I thought you might find helpful (Zauderer, 2023):

Statistic	Value
How many diapers will my baby use in the first year?	2,500-3,000
How many diapers will my baby use before potty trained?	7,000-8,000
What is the average cost to diaper my baby with disposable diapers for the first year?	$1,200-$2,000

How many diapers will my new baby use each day?	Between 10–12
What is the initial investment to kit your newborn in cloth diapers?	$450-$500
What will it cost me to launder those before my baby is potty trained?	On average, $325

You can clearly see that using cloth diapers saves a significant amount of cash and the environment. Today, there are so many types of cloth diapers to choose from, including different brands and materials. Understanding the cloth diaper terms like pockets, fitted, pre-folds, and wraps and selecting the best one for your budget and your child's comfort can feel overwhelming. You may need to try a couple of different types of cloth diapers to see what works best for you and your little one.

HYGIENE AND HEALTH TIPS

Let's discuss keeping your little bundle of joy clean and healthy while staying calm. We're exploring baby hygiene and health, but don't worry—it's all manageable. Here's the lowdown.

Cleaning Your Baby's Face, Head, Mouth, and Teeth

Before you start scrubbing, wash your hands—it's a golden rule. When it's time to clean up your baby's adorable face, dampen a soft washcloth with warm water. Gently wipe those baby blues from the inside corner out, using a fresh spot for each swipe. And remember, leave those cute little ears alone on the inside; just give them a gentle wipe on the outside.

For that baby hair, gently splash some warm water on their head. Then, pat dry with a soft towel, keeping the whole process as calm as a spa day. Use only plain water for newborn babies. You can switch to using unperfumed baby baths when they are around four to six weeks old, but be cautious and use only a small amount to avoid harming your baby's skin. If your baby has longer hair, you may need to use a small amount of mild shampoo on wet hair, lather it, and then rinse it off.

When it comes to dental hygiene, a simple water wipe-down after feeds will do the trick for those toothless grins. Once those pearly whites start peeking through, introduce a soft infant toothbrush for a gentle clean.

Nail and Umbilical Cord Care

Trimming those mini nails can feel like performing surgery, but with baby-safe scissors and a calm atmosphere, it is a breeze. Aim to snip during naptime or distract them with their favorite song.

Now, onto that tiny umbilical cord stump. Keep it clean and dry post-bath, avoiding diaper cover-ups to speed up the healing process. Diaper brands often have a handy cutout for this very reason. And remember, hands washed before handling!

Bathing Your Newborn

Two to three baths a week will keep your baby fresh as a daisy. But if they're loving the splash time, daily dips are okay, too. Just remember, too many baths can dry out that baby skin, so moderation is key.

Pick a relaxed moment for bath time—it's as much for you as it is for them. And as for location, anywhere warm, safe, and clean will do. The kitchen sink is a great spot in the early days, but as your mini-me grows, a plastic baby bath may steal the show.

Prep is everything, Dad. Before diving in, ensure all your supplies are within arm's reach—think towel, washcloth, and mild baby cleanser. And skip the soap; it's too harsh for delicate baby skin. Also, keep distractions like phones at bay for a smoother experience.

When it's showtime, start by gently easing them into the water, making sure to keep a firm grip. Cleanse away, starting with the face and neck and saving the best for last—those adorable tiny toes!

Once the bath is over, it's time for the drying and dressing marathon. Support their little heads as you lift them out of the water and onto a cozy towel. Pat them dry, paying special attention to those cute little creases. Then, dress them in their finest diaper and outfit before tucking them into a safe spot for some well-deserved rest.

Remember, Dad, practice makes perfect when it comes to baby bath time. So, take your time, stay calm, and enjoy those precious moments splish-splashing with your little one.

WHAT IF BABY IS SICK?

So, your little one isn't feeling their best? No worries; it happens to the best of us. Let's tackle these common baby hiccups together.

Why Does My Baby Need Extra Care?

When you bring your sweet little one home from the hospital, you will need to keep a close eye on them until they get a bit bigger. Their immune systems need a bit more time to build up and give them the protection they need. Keep an eye out for the following (*Newborn Illness*, 2023):

- Newborns face an increased risk of infections. They may show signs of illness at any time within the first month. It is important to closely monitor your baby, especially during the initial seven days of life.
- Newborns are more likely to get a blood infection (sepsis) and can become very sick fast. This is why you shouldn't ignore signs of illness in newborns.
- Newborns are eating machines. If your baby doesn't show an interest in feeding, call your doctor.
- If you notice a change in your baby's facial features, skin, coloring, or breathing, call immediately.

Ear Infections, Colds, Sore Throats, Colic, Digestive Problems, Skin Rashes, and Allergies

Babies, bless their little hearts, are still getting used to this big, wide world, so it's no surprise they might pick up a bug or two along the way. If your baby is under three months old and seems off, don't hesitate to call the doctor. Better safe than sorry, right?

Now, for the older munchkins, a common cold usually doesn't warrant a doctor's visit. But hey, if you're unsure or things seem to be getting worse, it's never a bad idea to give your pediatrician a buzz.

If you suspect an ear infection or a sore throat, notice an unusual rash, or see a change in the feeding habits of your newborn, it is important to call the doctor immediately. It is always better to err on the side of caution.

Listen to the advice given by your doctor before relying on advice from family or friends. They mean well, and those helpful tips may have worked for them, but each baby comes with their own set of unique issues and should be treated as such.

Fever Fighters

Now, about those fevers, they're like your baby's bodyguards, fighting off the bad guys. But if your little one's not feeling too hot (literally), you can use infant or children's fever reducers like acetaminophen or ibuprofen to help them feel more comfy. Do not use acetaminophen under 12 weeks of age unless your pediatrician advises.

When to Hit the Panic Button

Now, don't go full-on panic mode, but keep an eye out for any red flags. There are situations that warrant an immediate need for medical intervention. Give your doctor a call right away if there are any of the following signs:

- Changes in feeding routines, like waking up for feeds or leaving them unfinished
- Sweating excessively while feeding
- Any indications of sickness such as vomiting, coughing, or diarrhea
- If your baby looks pale or bluish

- Swollen fontanelle (soft spot) on the crown of the head
- Sleeping far more than usual and being lethargic
- Fever in an infant younger than 12 weeks—important: Do *not* give your baby any fever medication before consulting a healthcare provider
- If you believe your child needs immediate medical attention

Remember, you've got this, Dad! And if in doubt, don't hesitate to reach out for support.

FEEDING FUNDAMENTALS

Whether you're diving into breastfeeding, jumping into formula, or gearing up for solid foods down the road, there are a few things to keep in mind.

Supporting your partner in breastfeeding is crucial from the start. Sure, you might not be the one with the milk factory, but you're still an important player in this game. Here's how you can step up to the plate:

- **Be a jack of all trades:** You might not have the milk, but you've got the magic touch. You can soothe, bathe, change, dress, cuddle, and burp that baby. Don't underestimate your powers here.
- **Keep an eye out for hunger signals:** Learn the baby's cues for hunger so you can swoop in and deliver them to your partner for feeding time. It's like playing detective but with a much cuter suspect.

- **Guard the fortress:** Your home is now a sanctuary for baby and momma bear. Limit those visitors to give your partner the rest she deserves. Trust me, everyone will understand.
- **Step up your chore game:** It's time to channel your inner domestic hero. Cook, clean, do laundry—you name it. And if your partner needs something while she's breastfeeding, do your best to get it for her.
- **Sprinkle some encouragement:** Boost your partner's spirits by being her biggest cheerleader. Remind her she's doing an amazing job because, let's face it, she totally is.

Remember, this is a team effort. By supporting your partner in breastfeeding, or whatever choice of feeding you both make, you're not just feeding your baby; you're nurturing your family bond.

How Often Is My Baby Going to Eat?

Understanding your baby's feeding needs is crucial whether you're just starting this journey or knee-deep in diaper duty. Here's a no-nonsense breakdown for each stage (Christiano, 2023):

- **Up to 2 weeks of life:** In these early days, your tiny human is just figuring out how this eating thing works. Expect them to take in about 0.5 ounces of formula or breast milk per feeding in the first few days, then gradually increase to around 13 ounces.
- **2 weeks–2 months:** As your baby grows, so does their appetite. They'll likely start taking in 2–4 ounces per feeding during this phase. It's a bit of a guessing game, but trust your instincts and your baby's cues.

- **2–4 months:** By now, your little munchkin is getting the hang of this feeding business. They'll typically consume 4–6 ounces per feeding. Keep those bottles and burp cloths handy!
- **4–6 months:** Time to introduce some solids into the mix! Alongside 24–36 ounces of formula or breast milk a day, start incorporating 1–4 tablespoons of cereal, fruits, and veggies into their diet. It's like a mini food adventure for your tiny explorer!
- **6–8 months:** As your baby becomes more of a gourmet diner, aim for 24–36 ounces of formula or breast milk, spread out over 4–6 nursing sessions. Introduce more solids like cereals, fruits, veggies, and even a bit of protein like yogurt or crumbled egg.
- **9–12 months:** Your little foodie is almost a toddler! Keep up with 16–30 ounces of formula or milk alongside a balanced diet of grains, fruits, veggies, dairy, and protein-packed foods.

Remember, every baby is different, so don't stress too much about exact amounts. Pay attention to your baby's cues, and trust that you'll figure it out together.

SOLUTIONS FOR TYPICAL NEWBORN CONCERNS

Let's dive into some of those typical hiccups you might encounter with your little bundle of joy. We're talking colic, jaundice, and SIDS.

Colic: What's the Deal?

So, you've got a colicky baby on your hands? First, take a deep breath. It's tough, but you've got this. Your baby might be crying for what seems like forever, at least three hours a day, three days a week. You'll notice their face turning a bit red, legs curling up, and fists clenched, almost like they're in pain. They might even be tooting up a storm and having trouble passing stool. It's like a mini tornado of stress for both of you.

What Causes It?

The truth is, nobody's entirely sure. It's like the mystery flavor of parenthood. However, theories range from gas to a sensitive digestive system. Some even think it's just your little one adjusting to this wild ride called life.

What Can I Do?

Alright, let's talk damage control. Try out different calming positions. Think about gentle rocking or holding them close. A gentle baby massage could also have a wonderful effect. And hey, maybe consider their birth. Sometimes, a traumatic entrance into the world can make them a bit stressed out. Why not give that skin-to-skin a try?

Jaundice: The Yellowing Conundrum

Now, onto jaundice. You'll notice the yellow tint, maybe in their eyes, mouth, or even their tiny hands and feet. This happens because babies have an abundance of red blood cells, and when those bad boys break down, they leave behind bilirubin, giving your little one that golden glow (Ansong-Assoku & Ankola, 2023).

What Can I Do?

Treatment isn't usually needed unless the bilirubin levels are through the roof. Just keep an eye on it and chat with your healthcare team if you're worried. If the baby requires treatment, their liver will process bilirubin effectively within a few days. Phototherapy is the usual treatment for moderate jaundice. Phototherapy changes the bilirubin in the baby's skin into a safer substance. Your baby might need to be undressed and placed in a warm, enclosed incubator under blue lights (Ansong-Assoku & Ankola, 2023).

SIDS: The Scary Unknown

Alright, let's tackle the big one: sudden infant death syndrome (SIDS). It tends to lurk in the shadows of parenthood with its unknown causes.

Prevention Tactics

Here's the lowdown on keeping your little one safe: Back is the safest position for your baby to sleep. Always place your baby on their back for sleep. Think feet to foot, and position them so their tootsies are at the end of their crib. Keep their head uncovered, and for the first four months, have them snooze in your room: no pillows, no thick blankets, no problem. And if you're bed-sharing, keep it clear of other kids and pets.

Creating a Safe Sleep Space

Last but not least, let's talk about creating the ultimate snooze zone for your baby. Back to sleep, firm mattress, no fluffy extras, and if possible, breast is best.

Alright, partner, you've got the basics down. Parenthood is a wild ride, but with a little know-how and a whole lot of love, you'll keep baby safe with ease.

INTERACTIVE ELEMENT: BABY CARE TRACKER

Ready to conquer the world of parenting one diaper at a time? Let's get started with your trusty daily baby care tracker. Here's a handy chart to keep everything in check. Feel free to reset daily:

Activity	Time	Details/notes
Diaper changes 1. 2. 3. 4. 5. 6. 7. 8. 9. 10.		
Feedings		

Health notes		

Now, onto the baby-proofing checklist. Let's turn your home into a fortress of safety:

Baby-proofing item	Completed?	Notes/additional measures
Outlet covers	Yes	
Corner guards	Yes	
Safety gates	Yes	
Cabinet/toilet locks	Yes	
Furniture anchors	Yes	
Cord shorteners	Yes	

Check off each activity as you go, and feel free to add any personal notes or additional safety measures you think of along the way.

We've covered a lot of ground in this chapter, from perfecting the diaper change sprint to mastering the art of bathing your little one.

Now, it's time to put all this wisdom into action. Get hands-on with your baby and dive into the messy, magical world of parenthood. Don't worry about being perfect; just being there for your baby is what matters most.

As we move forward, keep that excitement alive because in the next chapter, we're exploring your baby's sleep patterns, emotional milestones, and all those adorable developmental stages. Get ready to unlock more parenting superpowers and watch your little one blossom right before your eyes!

CHAPTER 4
SUPPORTING GROWTH AND DEVELOPMENT

Welcome to the fourth stage of the D.A.D.S. G.U.I.D.E. Framework. Did you know that around six months, babies begin to develop a sense of object permanence? Yep, that means they start realizing that just because something is out of sight, it doesn't mean it's gone for good. How does this change the way you play and interact with your child? Well, get ready to find out because we're about to tackle all there is to know about nurturing your baby's development.

From deciphering those mysterious sleep patterns to understanding those adorable little emotional milestones, I've got you covered. This chapter is not just about watching your baby grow; it's about actively participating in every step of the process. Because let's face it, there's nothing quite like being there for those first smiles, steps, and everything in between.

DECODING BABY'S SLEEP PATTERNS

Unlock the mysteries of your baby's sleep cycles and become the sleep whisperer you never knew you could be! Not only will you crack the code to less frustration and exhaustion, but you'll also be the hero of your baby's cognitive development. Who knew sleep could be so powerful?

So, here's the scoop on those mysterious sleep patterns (Pacheco, 2023):

Newborns (0–2 months):

- These little bundles of joy are basically professional sleepers, clocking in around 16–20 hours of shut-eye in their first four to six weeks. Jealous yet?

- Day and night? What's the difference? Newborns split their sleep time right down the middle.
- Expect their sleep to come in two- to three-hour stretches for breastfed babies and three- to four-hour stretches for those on the bottle.

Babies (3–6 months):

- Alright, they're getting a bit older now, but they still love their sleep, logging around 14 hours a day.
- About 8–9 hours of that time is going to get broken up by feedings. It's like they have a built-in alarm clock!
- Oh, and they're likely to squeeze in three naps throughout the day, each lasting about two hours.

Babies (6–12 months):

- These little explorers are still clocking in around 14 hours a day, but now they might manage a solid eight to nine hours without interruptions if they're well-fed.
- Naps? Yup, they're still on the agenda. Expect two or three of them, ranging from quick 30-minute power naps to more leisurely 2-hour siestas.

Toddlers (12+ months):

- The toddler stage, where sleep can sometimes feel like a distant dream for parents. They're looking at around 12–14 hours of sleep a day now.
- Nighttime sleep might settle around 10 hours straight if you're lucky.

- Naps? Well, they might still sneak in one of those, totaling around two to three hours.

So, there you have it; baby sleep cycles demystified. Just remember, every baby's a bit different, so don't stress too much if yours doesn't follow the textbook. Embrace the chaos, and try and grab those z's whenever you can!

Practical Tips to Establish a Sleep Routine

Alright, let's talk about getting your little one into a sleep routine before those bags under your eyes become permanent. First off, teaching your baby the difference between night and day is key.

During the day, let the sunlight flood in, play some fun games, and don't stress too much about regular noises when they're napping. But when it's nighttime, it's time to switch gears.

Here are some tips to help you create that soothing nighttime vibe:

- Keep the lights nice and low. Think cozy and soothing.
- Keep the chitchat to a minimum and speak in your best library voice.
- Once your little one is fed and changed, gently tuck them into bed.
- Only change diapers if it's absolutely necessary. We're aiming for minimal disruptions.
- As tempting as it may be, save the playtime for the daytime. Nighttime is all about quiet and sleep.

By sticking to these nighttime rituals, your baby will catch on that it's time for some shut-eye. Now, let's talk about crafting that perfect bedtime routine to cement the deal.

Start by giving your munchkin a relaxing bath, slip them into their comfiest jammies and a fresh diaper, then cozy them up in bed. A bedtime story is always a winner, followed by dimming the lights for that serene atmosphere. Shower them with goodnight kisses and cuddles, maybe hum a lullaby or switch on that trusty musical mobile. And hey, if they're at the teeth-brushing stage, go for it! Every routine is unique, so find what works for you and your little snoozer.

Real-Life Stories of Dads Who Faced Sleep Challenges

In the bustling city of sunny Los Angeles resides Mike, a man on the brink of exhaustion due to sleep deprivation. Picture this: The clock strikes the wee hours of the night, his infant wide awake, and Mike desperately grasping to keep his eyes open. In such dire circumstances, one must resort to unconventional methods, wouldn't you agree? And so, what does Mike do? He reaches for the reliable old duct tape. Yes, you read correctly. With the resolve of a father on a crucial mission, he expertly wraps his little one in a cozy blanket. And when that pint-sized escape artist attempts to wriggle free, Mike swiftly employs the tape to ensure that his bundle of joy remains snug as a bug. And behold, it worked like magic! The household finally enjoyed some much-needed rest, and Mike rightfully secured a shining gold star in the prestigious Dad Hall of Fame for his truly ingenious solution.

Now, let's jet over to the bustling streets of Baltimore, where Drew, our fearless dad warrior, is battling sleep deprivation like a champ. In a caffeine-fueled frenzy, he mistook a piece of toast for his phone, engaging in an intense conversation with it before realizing his mistake. Attempting to change his newborn's diaper, Drew ended up putting it on backward, resulting in a diaper fashion statement worthy of a dad award. In a moment of sheer exhaustion, he even tried to microwave an oven mitt instead of his cup of coffee, only to discover the error when his coffee was still ice cold. With each comical misstep, Drew's sleep-deprived antics became the stuff of legend in the journey of fatherhood.

You should take comfort in the fact that you're not alone in your sleep-deprived state. Whether you're resorting to duct tape or mistaking an oven mitt for a cup of coffee, remember that this, too, shall pass. And hey, who knows, maybe one day you'll look back on these sleepless nights and laugh!

RECOGNIZING EMOTIONAL MILESTONES

Let's explore the emotional milestones your baby will experience in their first year. Did you know the journey of emotional development starts soon after birth?

During the first six months, your new baby will mostly react in the moment, showing emotions based on what's happening right then. But as they hit the seventh month, things get interesting. This is when feelings like fear and anger start to show up, adding a new twist to your parenting.

As your baby hits the eight- to eleven-month mark, get ready for some serious judgment skills! They'll be super sensitive to what they like and don't like. Plus, separation anxiety might peak, making it tough to leave for work!

Saying goodbye to the baby days, your little one hits a milestone at their first birthday. They start talking and expressing their feelings. Get ready for some deep chats, even if it's mostly about bubbles or Mr. Bear!

How to Recognize and Respond to Cues

Alright, let's chat about getting your baby to feel cozy and connected with you. It's all about forming that strong emotional bond—what we call attachment. When babies trust that their caregivers (that's you and your partner) will be there to comfort them when they're upset, they feel safe and secure. And when they feel safe, they're more curious and ready to explore their world with confidence.

So, how do we make sure our new bundle feels as snug as a bug in a rug? Well, it starts with tuning in to their emotions and needs. Babies have their own unique way of expressing themselves, whether it's through cries, wiggles, or little facial expressions. As you spend time with your baby, you'll become great at reading their signals and responding in the right way.

It is important to know that you can't spoil a baby. Nope, it's not possible. I understand many of us grew up in a generation who were "put down" in order to prevent being spoiled. Our parents were taught that coddling, cuddling, or just holding your child too often had a negative effect. The research is in, and this isn't the case. Your little one is not manipulating you when they cry for attention; they're just communicating (*Connecting With Your Baby's Emotions*, n.d.).

Regardless of your baby's temperament, your job is to be the calm, patient rock they can rely on. Yep, you're their first emotional coach. As they grow, you'll help them learn to manage their feelings and move through the big, wide world.

Your baby might have their own unique style of communicating. Maybe they turn away when they need a breather or throw a tantrum in the grocery store when it's all a bit too much. Paying attention to these signals and responding with care lets your little one know they're heard and loved.

Remember, it's all about building that trust and connection, one snuggle at a time.

NAVIGATING DEVELOPMENTAL STAGES

Babies are like tiny sponges, soaking up knowledge and skills faster than you can imagine. They're not just growing physically but also mentally and emotionally. Here's a breakdown of what you can expect in those crucial developmental stages (Morin, 2022):

By two months:

- **Emotional and social:** Your baby starts to recognize faces and respond with those adorable smiles. They may even calm down when you speak to them or hold them.
- **Communication and language:** Besides crying, they start making other sounds and react to loud noises.
- **Physical development:** They begin to lift their head when lying on their tummy and make basic arm and leg movements.

By four months:

- **Emotional and social:** Prepare for spontaneous smiles and even some giggles. Your baby starts to actively engage with you by making sounds or reaching for things.
- **Communication and language:** They'll start cooing and making sounds in response to your conversations.

- **Physical development:** This is when they might start reaching for objects and rolling over. They can also hold their head up independently.

By six months:

- **Emotional and social:** Your baby becomes more aware of familiar faces and may even enjoy looking at themselves in the mirror.
- **Communication and language:** They'll start taking turns in making sounds with you and might even blow raspberries.
- **Physical development:** Rolling over both ways and sitting with some support are common milestones at this stage.

By nine months:

- **Emotional and social:** Stranger anxiety might kick in, and they'll show various facial expressions to express their feelings.
- **Communication and language:** Get ready for some adorable babbling and gestures like lifting arms to be picked up.
- **Cognitive development:** They'll start looking for objects that they can't see and enjoy simple games like peekaboo.

By twelve months:

- **Emotional and social:** Your baby starts engaging in simple games with you and might express emotions more clearly, including crying when you leave.

- **Communication and language:** They'll begin to wave goodbye, say simple words like "Mama" or "Dada," and understand basic commands like "no."
- **Cognitive development:** They'll show signs of problem-solving, like looking for hidden objects, and may even try to put things into containers.
- **Physical development:** This is when they might take their first steps while holding onto furniture and refine their fine motor skills, like using their thumb and pointer finger to pick up small objects.

Remember, all babies are individuals, so don't stress if your little one isn't hitting all these milestones right on schedule. However, if you have concerns, it's always a good idea to chat with your child's healthcare provider. They're there to support you and your baby.

How to Support These Stages

From day one, we're crucial players in our child's growth.

Playtime isn't just fun and games; it's the real deal for our baby's mental and physical development. We're talking about interactive, engaging play where we're front and center. But remember, it's not just structured play that counts. Every moment, from changing diapers to dinner, is an opportunity for our baby to learn and grow.

Babies see everything as playtime. Yep, even the mundane stuff is a chance for them to explore and learn.

Now, let's talk about sleep. Quality snooze time is key for our baby's development. So, anything we can do to help them sleep better is good for them.

SUPPORTING GROWTH AND DEVELOPMENT 75

But, on occasion, especially with breastfed babies, we might feel like our only job is to entertain. Be mindful that play is just as crucial as feeding. It's vital for every aspect of your baby's development.

Studies back this up. When we're more involved in playtime from the get-go, our babies perform better on cognitive tests down the road (*New Dads' Guide*, 2020). Plus, it's not just about them because bonding with our babies through playtime is pretty awesome for us, too.

So, what are some playtime hacks? Well, let's start with tummy time. It's like the gateway to all other developmental milestones. Start early, even from day one, and build up gradually.

It is also important to talk to your baby. Yeah, it might feel a bit silly at first, but they love it. Narrate your day, and ask them questions. They eat that stuff up.

Now, when it comes to choosing playtime, be strategic. Pick times when both you and your baby are at your best. Let's say mornings are when you have a break in your day, and baby is most alert. Perfect! But hey, find what works for you and your little one.

Oh, and don't overwhelm them with toys. Focus on one activity at a time, spread toys out, and rotate them to keep things fresh.

When your baby achieves something new, celebrate it! Praise them with a big smile and an excited voice. It'll encourage them to keep pushing those boundaries.

And let's not forget about reading. Yup, even with tiny tots, it's a big deal. It boosts their language skills, sharpens their minds, and hey, turning those pages is great for their motor skills too.

Now, let's talk about diaper changes. Sure, they're not the most glamorous moments, but they're prime learning opportunities. You can narrate what it is you are doing and sneak in a game or two of peek-a-boo.

Do your best to limit phone time during play. We don't want anything distracting our babies from all that important exploration.

Biggest Mistakes Dads Make When It Comes to Play and Development

Here are some common mistakes dads tend to make and some insider tips to help you navigate this exciting journey:

- **Mistake 1:** Believing that your actions don't matter for their growth? Think again! Even if your baby prefers chewing their foot over your tower of cups, your interactions are molding their world. Stay engaged, and you'll witness the impact unfold gradually.
- **Mistake 2:** Not doing tummy time because your baby isn't a fan? While it may not be their top pick initially, tummy time is key for their physical growth and development. Get on their level, chat with them, and offer some encouragement. They'll warm up to it eventually!
- **Mistake 3:** Neglecting to clean or sterilize toys? While you don't have to be a germaphobe, a little toy TLC can keep your kiddo in tip-top shape. A sprinkle of cleaning or a dash of sterilizing every now and then can work wonders!
- **Mistake 4:** Refrain from being the turbo engine behind your child's progress. While we're all eager for our little ones to reach those milestones, remember, even race cars

need pit stops. Allow them to enjoy their journey, set their own speed, and avoid revving up their development.
- **Mistake 5:** Not giving your child a gentle nudge? Sometimes, a little challenge can do wonders! Place toys slightly out of reach to spark their curiosity and encourage exploration. If they hit a roadblock, offer comfort and switch up the game plan.
- **Mistake 6:** Not allowing your wee one some alone time. It's natural to want to spend every waking moment with your baby, but giving them the freedom to play alone is key for development. It helps them gain independence and the capability to soothe themselves.
- **Mistake 7:** Not bothering to baby-proof your home? Ensure your space is safe for your little explorer. Baby-proofing not only prevents accidents but also grants them the freedom to roam without needing your watchful eye all the time.
- **Mistake 8:** Too much playing right before bed. Setting a peaceful vibe before hitting the hay is crucial for quality sleep. Cut back on exciting playtime right before bedtime to help them relax and catch much-needed sleep.
- **Mistake 9:** When they get hurt, don't play the blame game. Accidents happen, so cut yourself some slack. Instead, focus on giving them comfort and care when they need it most.

Now, here are a few bits of wisdom that nobody may have told you yet:

- The fanciest toy isn't always the best. Sometimes, simple objects like boxes or household items like pots and big spoons can be just as entertaining.

- Babies love contrasting colors, so don't underestimate the power of black-and-white patterns.
- Keep trying activities like peek-a-boo, even if they don't seem interested at first. Their preferences can change quickly.
- As they grow, be prepared for mini-tantrums. It's a sign of their growing independence, but they'll usually get distracted soon enough.
- You'll soon become an expert at deciphering your baby's cries. Trust your instincts and learn to differentiate between genuine needs and simple whines.

There you have it, Dad. Embrace the journey of play and development with your little one, and remember, you're doing great!

INTERACTIVE GROWTH CHART FOR YOUR BABY'S FIRST YEAR

Keeping track of your baby's growth is not only exciting but also essential for ensuring they're developing well. Here's a handy growth chart to help you monitor your little one's progress during their first year.

Instructions:

1. **Height:** Measure your baby's height from head to toe and record it in inches or centimeters.
2. **Weight:** Weigh your baby and note it down in pounds or kilograms.

3. **Head circumference:** Using a soft measuring tape, measure around the widest part of your baby's head and jot down the measurement.
4. **Pediatrician visits:** Make sure to attend all scheduled pediatrician appointments. They will also measure your baby's growth and provide guidance. Take note of the date and anything discussed here.

Growth Chart:

Age (months)	Height (in/cm)	Weight (lbs/kg)	Head Circumference (in/cm)	Pediatrician visits
1				
2				
3				
4				
5				
6				
7				
8				
9				
10				
11				
12				

Tips:

- Remember, every baby grows at their own pace, so don't stress too much about specific numbers.
- If you notice any significant deviations from the expected growth patterns or have concerns, don't hesitate to discuss them with your pediatrician.
- Enjoy these precious moments with your little one as they grow and develop before your eyes!

Tracking your baby's growth is just one of the many ways you're rocking fatherhood.

You've now equipped yourself with the essential knowledge to support your baby's growth and development. From understanding milestones to fostering a stimulating environment, you're laying the groundwork for your child's future success.

Now, let's bring these ideas to life! Seize the moment to interact with your baby every day, whether it's through playtime, reading, or just enjoying quality time together. Your active participation is key to their growth and development.

In the upcoming chapter, we'll dive into mastering the twists and turns of your relationships while juggling fatherhood. Brace yourself to amp up the connection with your partner and family as you evolve with your little sidekick.

CHAPTER 5
GROWING RELATIONSHIPS AND OVERCOMING CHALLENGES

We are moving into the fifth stage of the D.A.D.S. G.U.I.D.E. Framework. Bringing a tiny human into the world has a knack for shaking up your life in ways you never imagined. One area where you might be feeling the shift most keenly is in your relationships—both with your partner and with extended family.

Let me hit you with a question to ponder: How does the arrival of a baby change the dynamics of your romantic relationship, and what steps can you take to keep the love alive? Deep stuff, right? In this chapter we're diving deep into this topic.

Becoming a dad doesn't come with a manual, but if it did, this chapter would be a highlighted section. By the time you finish this chapter, you'll be armed with practical tools to keep the love alive with your partner amid the chaos of babyhood. Plus, we'll throw in some financial wisdom because, let's face it, those tiny diapers come with a not-so-tiny price tag.

MANAGING DIFFICULT BEHAVIORS

In earlier chapters, we discussed how to soothe your new baby in those first days and months you bring them home. We covered strategies that could help you become the baby whisperer you were meant to be. As your baby grows into a toddler, you can expect those tiny cries to turn into tantrums.

Yes, those ear-splitting, nerve-wracking moments that make you question everything. But don't worry, understanding and managing tantrums is all about having a game plan.

First off, let's decode tantrums. Picture this: Your little one is in meltdown mode, but why? It could be fear, frustration, anger, or sensory overload. Tantrums are their way of saying, "Hey, I can't handle this!" They're not intentionally trying to drive you up the wall; it's just their way of dealing with big emotions.

So, how do we tackle these tantrums head-on? Step one: Figure out what sets them off. Is it bedtime battles, hunger woes, or transitions from fun to not-so-fun stuff? Knowing the triggers is half the battle won.

Tantrums often become a habit. If they see it gets results (like getting a yummy treat or snagging extra screen time), they'll keep at it. That is where you come in, Dad. You've got to help them unlearn this tantrum tornado and replace it with better coping skills.

When tantrums strike, your response is key. Resist the urge to cave in or lose your cool. Ignoring the outburst (when it's safe to do so) and praising good behavior instead sends a powerful message: Tantrums won't get them what they want.

Stay cool as a cucumber. Seriously, losing your cool won't help anyone. Take a breather if you need to. Model the calm you want to see in them.

And remember, Dad, clear communication is key. Set clear expectations and praise them when they meet them. It's not about "behave yourself," it's about specifics like "stay seated during meals." Concrete goals make for smoother sailing.

So there you have it, Dad. Tantrums might feel like a storm you can't weather, but with understanding, patience, and a dash of calm, you've got this.

Real-Life Examples

Jack and the Power of Distraction

Jack was over the moon when his little bundle of joy arrived. He couldn't wait to cuddle, coo, and play with his newborn daughter. But soon, he realized that along with the sweetness, there came the occasional sour—the tantrums, the crying fits, and the all-out meltdowns that seemed to strike at the most inconvenient times.

One particularly memorable episode happened during a family gathering. Jack's daughter decided that naptime was overrated and opted for a full-blown meltdown instead. While wailing and flailing limbs flew, Jack felt his stress levels skyrocketing. But instead of joining the chaos, he took a deep breath and remembered a tip he'd picked up: distraction.

Jack scooped up his daughter and whisked her away from the noisy crowd. He found a quiet corner and pulled out her favorite toy. Sure enough, the tears dried up as she focused on the colorful shapes and sounds. Crisis averted.

From that day on, Jack learned the power of distraction in managing difficult behaviors. Whether it's a favorite toy, a silly face, or a funny noise, sometimes all it takes is a little diversion to calm the storm.

The Walmart Tantrum

In a bustling Walmart aisle, a father found himself facing a parenting predicament as his young son unleashed a tempest of emotions over a denied book purchase. Passersby might have paused to observe the unfolding drama, but it was the father's measured response that truly caught the attention of onlookers.

With a steadying hand and a calm demeanor, the father guided his distraught son to a quieter corner. There, under the hum of fluorescent lights and the faint scent of retail, he initiated a dialogue designed to soothe the storm raging within his child.

Taking a cue from the father's playbook, he began with a simple question, "Can you tell me where we are right now?" To which the boy, still sniffing back tears, responded with a shaky voice, "Walmart."

Encouraged, the father continued, gently probing, "And can you tell me what you are standing on?"

The boy hesitated for a moment before answering, "The floor."

The father continued, "Do you know if the floor is carpet or tile?" The boy, more calm now, responded, "Tile."

With each question, the father skillfully anchored his son to the present, redirecting his attention away from the whirlwind of emotions and toward the tangible reality of their surroundings. By engaging the boy's senses, the father was able to guide him back from the brink of a meltdown.

Witnessing this scene unfold, bystanders marveled at the father's composure and patience. His ability to navigate his toddler's emotions without succumbing to frustration or anger was a testament to his unwavering dedication to his child's well-being.

In the eyes of onlookers, the father's actions spoke volumes. He wasn't just managing a difficult behavior; he was forging a deeper connection with his son, teaching him valuable lessons in emotional regulation and resilience.

Reflecting on the encounter, one observer remarked, "The father did an amazing job of calming down his child with a few intentional questions." It was a simple yet powerful reminder that sometimes, the most effective parenting strategies require little more than a steady hand and a compassionate heart.

MAINTAINING A STRONG ROMANTIC RELATIONSHIP

Let's talk about keeping the flames of romance burning bright, even in the chaos of newborn parenthood. Yeah, life changes big time when that little bundle arrives, but it doesn't mean you and your partner have to lose that loving feeling. Here's the lowdown on keeping the romance alive post-baby:

- **Talk it out:** Communication is key. Whether you're feeling frustrated, overwhelmed, or just plain tired, don't bottle it up. Share your feelings with your partner. Be real about what you need and why. And hey, carve out some time each day to focus solely on each other, even if it's just for a quick chat.
- **Date night, anyone?:** Remember those spontaneous dinners and outings? Yeah, they might be a rare treat now, but that doesn't mean date night is off the table. Plan ahead, book a babysitter, and make time for some quality couple time. And if going out feels like too much effort, no worries—schedule a cozy night in together.
- **Show some love:** Running the baby gauntlet can leave you both feeling drained. Don't forget to show appreciation for all the little things your partner does, from changing diapers to tackling that never-ending pile of laundry. A little gratitude goes a long way.

- **Me time matters:** It's easy to lose yourself in babyland, but don't forget to carve out some time for yourself, too. Whether it's catching up on your favorite show or just chilling with a good book, self-care is crucial. A happier you makes for a happier relationship.
- **Get intimate:** Yeah, I know, the idea of sex might feel like a distant memory right now. But intimacy goes beyond the bedroom. Hold hands, cuddle up on the couch—whatever makes you both feel connected. Just remember, it's all about finding what works for both of you.
- **Keep laughing:** When all else fails, don't forget to laugh. Parenthood is a wild ride, so keep a sense of humor handy. Share a joke, reminisce about the good times, and remember to enjoy the journey together.

Fatherhood might be a crazy ride, but with a little effort and a whole lot of love, you and your partner can keep that romance alive and kicking.

Tips for Date Nights, Communication, and Shared Responsibilities

Balancing diapers, late-night feedings, and work can leave your romantic life feeling a bit like a distant memory. I've got some practical tips to help you keep the love alive:

- **Show genuine interest in your partner:** It's easy to get caught up in the whirlwind of baby duties, but don't forget to check in with your partner. Ask about their day, their thoughts, and their feelings. Show them that you value their perspective and that they're still a priority in your life.

- **Communicate understanding:** Parenthood can be stressful, and sometimes tensions can run high. When conflicts arise, strive to understand where your partner is coming from. Listen actively, empathize with their feelings, and work together to find solutions.
- **Offer support:** Being a new parent is tough, and your partner needs your support now more than ever. Whether it's lending a hand with diaper changes, giving them a break for some much-needed self-care, or simply being a shoulder to lean on, show up for them in any way you can.
- **Create solidarity:** Parenthood is a team effort, so make sure you're on the same page with your partner. Discuss your parenting goals, values, and strategies, and work together as a united front.
- **Show similarities:** Parenthood can sometimes highlight differences between partners, but it's important to focus on the things you have in common. Celebrate your shared interests, values, and goals, and let those moments of connection strengthen your bond.
- **Show affection:** Don't let intimacy fall by the wayside. Even if you're both exhausted, make time for cuddles, kisses, and physical affection. It's a powerful way to reaffirm your love for each other amid the chaos of parenting.
- **Help your partner to process:** Parenthood can bring up a lot of emotions, from joy and excitement to fear and anxiety. Be there for your partner as they navigate these feelings. Encourage open communication and let them know that it's okay to express themselves.
- **Listen first before suggesting solutions:** When your partner comes to you with a problem, resist the urge to jump straight into problem-solving mode. Instead, listen

attentively and validate their feelings before offering any advice or solutions.

Remember, maintaining a strong romantic relationship takes effort, especially in the midst of the chaos of new parenthood. But by prioritizing communication, support, and connection, you can keep the spark alive and weather any storm together. Take it one step at a time, give yourselves grace, and trust in the strength of your partnership.

RELATIONSHIPS WITH EXTENDED FAMILY

How exactly do you involve your extended family after baby arrives? You know, those eager grandparents and relatives who are probably dying to lend a hand. When you and your partner are feeling like you're drowning in baby duties, these people can be a lifesaver.

The first thing to remember is this is your baby and your family, and you need to do what works best for you. Some families and cultures believe in surrounding themselves with family from the minute baby comes home. Others like to have a week or two alone to bond with baby. Again, do what feels most comfortable for you and your family.

Bringing home a new baby does become overwhelming. Your entire focus falls on the baby, which means household duties fall by the wayside. So, if the family wants to help, why not delegate tasks?

Pick something around the house that your eager helper can handle without needing a whole manual. Maybe it's laundry duty or giving them a quick kitchen tour so they can help unload the dishwasher without needing to constantly ask where everything goes. Getting some extra hands on deck for chores is a game-changer. That laundry pile isn't getting any smaller by itself.

And hey, if they're up for it, let them babysit for a bit while you and your partner sneak off for a movie or a dinner date. If leaving the baby makes you nervous, no worries; they can send you updates or pictures to keep your mind at ease.

Another big one? Let them feed you. Yep, I'm serious. When your family offers to cook or bring food, don't be a hero—let them. It means you get to spend more time with your little one and actually eat a decent meal.

Now, when it comes to asking for help, don't be shy. Friends and family are usually itching to lend a hand if you just speak up. Some might be hesitant to offer assistance, thinking they'll intrude, so when you ask directly, it gives them the green light. You can let go of the guilt, thinking you are somehow failing at this parenting thing. Family is there to help, so let them.

Be mindful that sometimes, all that help comes with a side of unsolicited advice. You know the drill, the "You should do this" or "Babies shouldn't be held too much" comments. Remember, most of the time, they're just trying to help, even if it feels like they're critiquing your every move. If it starts getting under your skin, don't hesitate to set some boundaries early on. Like if the in-laws won't quit with the parenting pointers, a gentle reminder to give you some space can save you a lot of headaches down the road.

FINANCIAL AND HEALTHCARE PLANNING

It is time to chat about the not-so-glamorous but utterly essential aspects of financial and healthcare planning when you're stepping into the whirlwind world of fatherhood. Trust me, this stuff might not be as exciting as picking out baby names, but it's what's going to keep your ship steady as you navigate the choppy waters of parenthood.

First up, let's hit the wallet. Babies are adorable bundles of joy, but they also come with a price tag. You'll want to budget for essentials. My advice? Make a list, check it twice, and then maybe check it again because you'll probably forget something. Set a realistic budget and stick to it like glue. Babies have a knack for emptying your pockets faster than you can say "college fund."

Now, onto healthcare. This is no time to be playing roulette with your insurance plans. Take the time to understand your coverage options. Look into what's covered for prenatal care, labor and delivery, and those inevitable trips to the pediatrician's office. Don't forget to factor in any co-pays, deductibles, or out-of-pocket expenses. It's not the most thrilling read, but it beats getting blindsided by a hefty medical bill.

Oh, and childcare. Brace yourself, partner, because this one's a doozy. Whether you're considering daycare, a nanny, or leaning toward the stay-at-home parent route, do your homework. Research costs in your area, visit facilities, and ask for recommendations.

Bottom line: Money matters when you're bringing a tiny human into the world. Plan ahead, budget wisely, and don't be afraid to ask for help or advice from fellow parents who've been there, done that, and probably have the spit-up stains to prove it.

Budgeting for Baby Essentials

You might have heard all sorts of numbers thrown around, but no matter where you stand financially, that first year is going to shake up your wallet.

A recent survey showed that some people believe that the first year will be handled for about $5,000. Whether you're cruising on a comfy income or tightening those purse strings, that sweet bundle of joy is going to cost you much more (Renter, n.d.).

Let's dive into some numbers. Picture two different households: one's bringing in $40,000 a year, while the other's riding high on a $200,000 income. Now, the big bucks crew, they're probably splurging on things like life insurance and maybe even saving up for college. But for the $40k gang, those might not even be on the radar. Now, we crunched the numbers on stuff like food, housing, transportation, diapers, healthcare, and all those must-have baby items. And you know what we found? Even if you're bargain hunting like a pro and skipping out on things like life insurance and college savings, that first year with a new baby could still set you back as much as $21,248 on a $40,000 income (Renter, n.d.).

Many soon-to-be parents are banking on friends and family to help out. But reality check— 57% of current parents are kicking themselves for not getting their finances in line sooner. And their biggest regret? Not putting away enough for junior's college fund (Renter, n.d.).

So, let's clear the air on some misconceptions. It turns out that a lot of us are way off the mark on what it actually costs to raise a little one. And when it comes to specifics, well, we're not hitting the bullseye there either. Diapers might seem like a wallet-drainer, but they're actually not the biggest expense. Childcare? That's where the real chunk of change goes.

And hey, life insurance? It's not as pricey as some might think. So, when it comes to budgeting for baby, it pays to know where your dollars are really going.

Healthcare Costs

You can't have a baby without considering the costs. In the US, bringing a wee one into the world will set you back around $18,865, from the bun in the oven to the delivery room and even the after-party (Rivelli, 2023). If you're lucky enough to have health insurance, they'll foot most of the bill. But if you're not, get ready for a wallet workout when that hospital bill comes knocking.

The real price tag of bringing a new human into the world? Well, it's like a complicated math problem—it all boils down to how the baby decides to make their grand entrance and where in the world you are at that moment!

Want to know how to save a fortune on childbirth? Get health insurance!

Childcare Options

Okay, so we have broken down the costs to bring your baby into the world and take care of your partner. But what about the costs to care for your child if both parents work? Within the first five years of their child's life, parents are basically playing a never-ending game of financial limbo that even the most flexible accountant would struggle to navigate. A robust economy relies on parents being able to stash some cash and treat themselves, but with the monstrous burden of childcare expenses, those money-saving dreams are turning into a financial comedy sketch.

The U.S. Department of Health and Human Services thinks childcare is best when it costs families less than 7% of their household income. But get this: According to current surveys, parents are shelling out a whopping 24% of their household income on child care. 60% are forking over 20% or more, and a whopping 84% are dishing out 10% or more (Care.com Editorial Staff, 2021).

What is the national average of childcare costs?

In 2024, we've got nanny costs, babysitters, daycare, and family care centers all lined up by age and number of kids per week (Care.com Editorial Staff, 2021):

- **Cost of nannies per week:** $766 (up 4% from $736 in 2022)
- **Cost of daycares per week:** $321 (up 13% from $284 in 2022)
- **Cost of family care centers per week:** $230 (up 0.4% from $229 in 2022)
- **Cost of babysitters per week:** $192 (up 7% from $179 in 2022)

So, let's talk game plan. Do your homework! Figure out how much dough you need to stash away for the little one's grand entrance. Next up, chat about one parent taking time off to save money. Can you swing it? Maybe call in the reinforcements. Do Grandma and Grandpa want to be the MVP babysitters a couple of days a week? Get these talks rolling way before the baby arrives, and be ready for the adventure!

FAMILY RELATIONSHIP PLAN WORKSHEET

The following worksheet is here to help you maintain your romantic relationship and involve family members in the life of your new bundle. Feel free to reuse it whenever you need some inspiration.

Romantic Relationship Goals

Write down three goals you have for your relationship in the next month.

1.

2.

3.

Involving Extended Family Members

Write down your answers to the following questions.

What are three I could ask our parents to help with around the house to allow us more time together and with the baby?

1.
2.
3.

What three people in our extended family do we trust to babysit so we can enjoy a date night?

1.
2.
3.

Support System

Who can we call when we need added support?

Self-Care Plan

What are three things I can do to ensure my partner prioritizes self-care?

1.
2.
3.

What are three things I can do to ensure I prioritize self-care for me?

1.
2.
3.

The moral of the story is simple: plan, plan, and plan some more. To feel in control, remember to research and budget. Babies may not be cheap, but being prepared is priceless! Let's gear up for the next chapter. Armed with insights on nurturing relationships and handling parenting hurdles, you're all set to safeguard your growing family. In the upcoming chapter, we'll dive into creating a safe haven for your little adventurer!

MAKE A DIFFERENCE WITH YOUR REVIEW

My goal is to help another dad achieve his dream and make it feel more attainable.

I aim to make The First Time Dad Survival Guide easily accessible to new fathers and to provide guidance for their journey through fatherhood.

Most people judge books by their covers and reviews. A new dad needs your help.

If you find this book helpful and/or inspiring, please take a moment to leave a review:

Simply scan the QR code below:

I am thrilled to continue supporting you and your family. I believe you will find the upcoming strategies helpful!

Thank you from the bottom of my heart!

Now, let's get back to our adventure in Dad-Land.

H.S. Gray

CHAPTER 6
UPHOLDING SAFETY

Here, we are at the sixth stage of the D.A.D.S. G.U.I.D.E. Framework. You've probably heard the saying, home is where the heart is, but did you know it's also where a lot of accidents happen? Did you know that over 70% of child accidents happen in the home (Lock, 2021)? Yep, the home sweet home can sometimes turn into a hazard zone, especially when you've got a tiny explorer on the loose.

In this chapter, we're diving deep into the world of childproofing and safety measures to ensure your home remains a sanctuary of love and security for your new baby.

We're going to cover everything from the basics of childproofing to creating a nurturing environment that fosters growth and happiness. By the end of this chapter, you'll be equipped with the knowledge and confidence to provide a safe, supportive, and balanced haven for your family.

CHILDPROOFING ESSENTIALS

When your new baby arrives home, suddenly, you're in charge of keeping this tiny human safe. Childproofing your place becomes an important job. It's crucial because, let's face it, these little explorers are like tiny accident magnets. Safety first, right?

By slapping some cabinet locks, doorknob covers, and gates for stairs in place, and throwing in a dash of supervision, you can outsmart those tiny people and keep them from turning your home into an accident zone.

Here's your comprehensive guide to childproofing every nook and cranny of your home:

The living room:

- **Crawl test:** Get down on all fours and explore. Look for anything a curious crawler could grab, pull, or topple.
- **Edge guards:** Cover sharp corners of furniture with edge guards to protect against head bumps.
- **Secure furniture:** Bolt heavy furniture to the wall to prevent tipping.
- **Cable management:** Tame those wild cords and cables. Use cord organizers or hide them behind furniture.

The Kitchen:

- **Cabinet locks:** Install locks on cabinets containing cleaning supplies, sharp objects, or anything hazardous.
- **Stove guard:** Consider a stove guard to keep little hands away from hot surfaces.
- **Childproof latches:** Keep appliances like the dishwasher or oven off-limits with childproof latches.
- **Tablecloths:** Skip the tablecloth to prevent little ones from pulling down hot dishes or sharp objects.

The Bathroom:

- **Medicine cabinet lock:** Keep all medications, vitamins, and toiletries locked away.
- **Non-slip mats:** Prevent slipping accidents by placing non-slip mats in the tub and shower.
- **Toilet lock:** Install a toilet lock to prevent curious explorers from taking a dive head first.
- **Temperature control:** Set your water heater to a safe temperature of 120° Fahrenheit to avoid scalding.

The Bedroom:

- **Window guards:** Install window guards or safety locks to prevent falls.
- **Blind cords:** Keep blind cords out of reach, cut them, or use cord wind-ups to prevent strangulation.
- **Secure dressers:** Anchor dressers and bookshelves to the wall to prevent tipping.

General areas:

- **Outlet covers:** Cover all electrical outlets with safety plugs.
- **Door stoppers:** Use door stoppers to prevent little fingers from getting caught.
- **Gates:** Install safety gates at the top and bottom of stairs and in doorways to restrict access to hazardous areas.
- **Small objects:** Keep small objects like coins, batteries, magnets, and buttons out of reach to prevent choking hazards.

Emergency preparedness:

- **CPR training:** Take a pediatric CPR and first aid course to be prepared for emergencies.
- **Emergency contacts:** Keep a list of emergency contacts easily accessible, including pediatricians and poison control.
- **Fire safety:** Install smoke detectors and carbon monoxide detectors, and create a fire escape plan.

Remember, childproofing is an ongoing process. As your little one grows and becomes more mobile, you'll need to reassess and adjust your safety measures accordingly. Stay vigilant, and may the babyproofing force be with you!

Real-Life Safety Stories

Thomas and the Vitamins

Like any new dad, Thomas had grown accustomed to the delightful chaos that came with his two-year-old daughter, Riley. Her playful antics often left him amused, if not a tad frazzled, especially when they involved messes that seemed to defy logic (it's been said that having a toddler in the home is like turning on the blender and forgetting to put the lid on it).

Yet, within the daily whirlwind of toddlerhood, there were moments that struck a chord of parental concern in Thomas' heart.

One such heart-stopping incident unfolded when Thomas stepped out of the room momentarily—long enough to grab a drink from the kitchen—only to return and find Riley perched on her tiptoes, gleefully munching on vitamins he had unknowingly left within the little one's reach on their bedroom dresser.

Thomas was shocked because he didn't know Riley possessed the strength and determination to engineer such a daring escapade. Yet there she was, having executed a three-step plan with the precision of a seasoned acrobat: (1) lifting a hefty footstool, (2) strategically placing it in front of the dresser, and (3) reaching up to breach the supposedly child-resistant container housing the vitamins.

Miraculously, Riley's discerning taste buds spared her from eating the vitamins as she promptly spat them out. But the episode served as a stark reminder for Thomas. Despite his diligent efforts to childproof his home, he had overlooked the crucial aspect of medicine safety. Like many parents, he had assumed that certain items were inherently out of reach for curious little hands.

Marcus and the Magnets

Marcus, a diligent father, found himself facing a tense situation involving his three-year-old daughter. After she swallowed many small magnets from his desk toy, she was admitted to the hospital. X-rays revealed 12 magnets stuck in her abdomen. Despite multiple attempts to remove them during a medical procedure, the magnets shifted beyond reach.

Regrettably, the magnets were now stuck in a worse place, potentially leading to a bowel perforation. Although his daughter looked healthy, internally, she was at serious risk. Luckily, a specialist was able to use his skills to extract the magnets before any serious damage occurred, and emergency surgery was avoided.

Marcus and his family had no idea that magnets would cause such serious issues. This gave them a wake up call and his entire family continue to pass this education on to new parents.

Noah and the Fall

James experienced every parent's nightmare when his youngest child, Noah, fell out of the window at their home. The family had just returned from Noah's karate class, and while preparing dinner before taking their two older children to baseball, chaos ensued. With their three children, aged four, six, and eight, playing around the house, Noah had managed to construct a makeshift ladder out of blankets, pillows, and even his bathroom stool to reach the window.

James's partner heard Noah's panicked cries of "I'm stuck, I'm stuck!" and rushed to the room, only to find it empty with the window wide open. She screamed for James, who was in the middle of putting dinner in the oven. James found Noah on the concrete walkway outside with severe head injuries.

As both James and his partner were healthcare professionals, they knew it was bad. An ambulance arrived, and Noah was taken to the children's hospital.

Noah spent seven days in the pediatric intensive care unit with severe skull fractures and significant brain swelling and bleeding.

On day six, Noah woke up, his breathing tube removed, and James heard the soft word, "Daddy."

Today, Noah is home, recovering, playing energetically, and chatting away. He's still undergoing physical therapy, occupational therapy, and speech therapy, but James remains hopeful for his son's recovery despite the long road ahead.

This family emphasizes the unknown dangers of window safety. We tend to babyproof our homes when we bring a new baby home and then forget to adjust and revisit that plan as they grow.

It is recommended that once your child begins walking, take another look at what dangers could be lurking.

CREATING A LOVING HOME ATMOSPHERE

Let's talk about creating a warm and loving environment at home. It's not just about comfy couches and happy vibes; it's about setting up a solid foundation for your child. Get this right, and you're giving your kid a head start in life (Bishop, 2023):

- **Physical health:** When your home is filled with love, your kiddo's health tends to be top-notch. They're less likely to struggle with things like obesity because they pick up healthy eating habits and enjoy staying active.
- **Mental health:** Now, let's talk about the good stuff: mental health. Kids raised in loving homes are less likely to deal with heavy stuff like anxiety or depression. That's a win for their future happiness right there.
- **Brain power:** Besides the warm fuzzies, a loving home does wonders for your kid's brainpower. They tend to ace school and get creative easily. Plus, they're social butterflies, mastering things like managing feelings and making buddies.
- **Building resilience:** Ever seen a child bounce back from a fall like it's no big deal? That's resilience. When we acknowledge their feelings and give them comfort, they learn to tackle life's curveballs with confidence.
- **Mental health matters:** Pay attention to how your child is feeling. If they're not their usual self—maybe acting withdrawn or moody—it could be a sign they need some extra love and attention.

Remember, you and your partner are the ultimate emotional support squad for your little one. Spend quality time together, chat openly, and tune into their feelings.

Tips for Maintaining a Calm and Nurturing Atmosphere

Talk It Out

Keeping the chatter open and respectful sets up a solid foundation for a happy home. Keep it real with your partner and steer clear of shouting matches; it creates a space where our little one feels safe to speak up and be heard. That way, we're all in the loop, ready to tackle whatever life throws our way.

Hang Together

Bonding time is gold. Whether we're playing games, flipping through storybooks, or just taking a stroll, these moments strengthen your family ties. And hey, dinner together? It's the glue that keeps us connected through the day-to-day hustle.

Play Time, Anytime

Making room for play isn't just fun; it's essential. It's when our kids get to be wild and imaginative, and we get to be kids again, too. So, more play means more giggles and lasting memories—just what the home doctor ordered.

Spread the Love

Showing some love isn't just a bonus; it's a must. A hug here, a "great job" there—it's all about making sure our kids feel the love. When they know they're cherished, it bolsters their confidence, like building a cozy nest where they can thrive.

Emotional IQ

Teaching our little ones to ride the emotional rollercoaster with finesse is key. Helping them navigate feelings and keep their chin up when things get bumpy sets them up for a smoother ride through life's twists and turns. Plus, it keeps our own family ship sailing steady.

Lead the Happiness Charge

When you prioritize your own happiness, it sends a powerful message to the whole crew. By taking care of yourself and keeping a sunny outlook, you're showing your child how to rock this happiness thing. It's contagious, and it makes our home a haven of good vibes.

By nailing these home happiness essentials—talking it out, hanging together, playing, spreading the love, emotional coaching, and leading by happy example—you're setting the stage for an awesome family vibe. It's not just about our kids; it's about us, too, creating a space where we all thrive together.

WHAT DO THE PROFESSIONALS SAY?

Studies from Duke University Medical School have shown that affection from parents is like a superfood for your kid's well-being. We're talking about higher self-esteem, better grades, smoother communication, all the good stuff (Gardner, 2010).

Many studies have shown that children who were showered in affection turned out to be happier, less stressed adults, all thanks to a little hormone called oxytocin. It's like the love drug, and it's what makes that parent-kid bond so darn strong (Schwartz, 2017).

A study from UCLA jumped in on this love train, too. They found that unconditional love and affection can literally rewire your kid's brain for happiness and lower anxiety. They uncovered that all this love might just shield your child from the nasty effects of stress in adulthood (Rivero, 2013).

So, how do you make sure your home is a love-filled haven? It's simple, really. From day one, cuddle up with your baby. Rock them, hold them close, and let them feel your love. And as they grow, get creative! Dance parties, silly games, whatever gets those hugs flowing.

Just remember, balance is key. Respect your kid's boundaries as they grow, and adapt your affection to what they need. It's all about finding that sweet spot between love and space.

So go ahead, Dad, embrace the love. Your kid will thank you for it.

BALANCING PERSONAL DEVELOPMENT AND FATHERHOOD

It's easy to get lost in the whirlwind of diapers, feedings, and sleepless nights, but hey, you're still you, right? Here are some strategies to keep growing as a person while tackling this whole dad thing:

- **Set realistic goals:** Look, you're not going to become a marathon runner or write a novel in the first few months of fatherhood. Start small. Maybe it's reading a few pages of a book each night or going for a short walk during lunch break. Pick something achievable.
- **Prioritize self-care:** Yeah, I know, self-care sounds like something you'd hear in a spa commercial, but hear me out. Caring for yourself is not self-centered; it's essential. Grab a quick nap when the baby sleeps, eat something that isn't leftover pizza crusts, and, for the love of sanity, take a shower. You'll feel like a new man.

- **Make time for hobbies:** Remember those things you used to do before diapers took over your life? Whether it's playing guitar, tinkering with cars, or binge-watching cheesy action movies, carve out time for your hobbies.
- **Learn to say no (nicely):** Your boss wants you to work late? Your buddy wants you to join his fantasy football league? Learn to say no when it interferes with your family time or personal well-being. You don't have to be a people pleaser all the time.
- **Connect with other dads:** You're not in this alone. Sharing experiences and tips can be surprisingly refreshing.
- **Include your partner:** Parenthood isn't a solo gig. Involve your partner in your personal development journey. Maybe you can take turns watching the baby while the other hits the gym or pursues their interests. Supporting each other's growth makes you both better parents.
- **Embrace imperfection:** Let's face it, none of us have it all figured out. There will be days when you'll feel like you're failing at everything, and that is okay. Cut yourself some slack. As long as you're doing your best, you're doing just fine.

Remember, personal development isn't about becoming a flawless superhero; it's about becoming the best version of yourself, messy diapers and all. So go ahead, chase those dreams, take care of yourself, and rock this dad thing like a boss.

SELF-CARE TIPS FOR DADS

You're juggling a gazillion things, and sometimes it feels like there's barely enough time to breathe, let alone take care of yourself. But here's the deal: neglecting your own well-being is like driving on an empty tank—you're going to break down sooner or later.

So, here's the lowdown on keeping your sanity intact without losing your dad badge:

- **Sink into a soothing soak:** Have you ever tried soaking in a warm bath after a marathon of dad tasks? It's pure bliss. Toss in some Epsom salts or essential oils, dim the lights, and let the stress melt away. Seriously, when was the last time you treated yourself to a long soak?
- **Nature strolls:** Step out into the great outdoors. Even if you're in a bustling city, find a quiet time like dawn and take a walk without distractions. No phone, no music—just you and the world around you. It's a game-changer.
- **Pick up a new hobby:** Have you ever thought about trying your hand at something new? Whether it's painting, cooking up a storm, or even learning a new language, dive in. It's not just about killing time; it's about feeding your soul with something fresh and exciting.
- **Knead away stress:** Treat yourself to a massage. Whether you book a professional session or invest in a massage gun, it's a VIP ticket to relaxation town. Ah, the sweet relief of tension melting away!
- **Tune into tunes:** Music is magic, my friend. Craft a playlist of your all-time favorites and let the melodies work their charm. Need a suggestion? Rediscover some old classics—yeah, high school was eons ago, but those tunes still hit the spot.
- **Sneaky snooze:** Have you ever heard of power naps? They're like mini-recharges for your brain. Sneak in a quick 20–30 minute nap when you're feeling zonked. Can't

nap? Aim for a solid eight hours at night—it's non-negotiable.
- **Mindfulness mission:** Take a breather and dive into mindfulness and meditation. Start small, find a quiet spot, and focus on your breath. Need a nudge? Try out guided meditations—they're like a soothing balm for your frazzled mind.
- **Gratitude attitude:** Take a moment each day to count your blessings. It's not just about being cheesy—it's about rewiring your brain to focus on the good stuff, even when life gets messy.

INTERACTIVE ELEMENT: HOME SAFETY CHECKLIST

I have included this checklist for you to assess and childproof your home. Be mindful to review and recheck your home every six months.

1. Kitchen:

- Are sharp objects like knives and scissors stored safely out of reach?
- Are cabinet locks installed to prevent access to hazardous items and chemicals?
- Are stove knob covers in place to prevent accidental burns or gas leaks?

2. Living room:

- Are heavy furniture pieces secured to the wall to prevent tipping over?
- Are electrical outlets covered with safety plugs?
- Are window blind cords tied up high or cut to prevent strangulation?

3. Bedroom:

- Is the crib positioned away from windows, heaters, and cords?
- Are crib slats the appropriate distance apart (2–3 fingers width)?
- Are soft bedding items like pillows, blankets, and stuffed toys removed from the crib?

4. Bathroom:

- Are all medications, toiletries, and cleaning products stored securely in locked cabinets?
- Are water heater temperatures set below 120 °F (48 °C) to prevent scalding?
- Are toilet lids kept down and locked to prevent drowning accidents?

5. General safety:

- Are smoke detectors installed on every floor of the house, and are they working properly?
- Are carbon monoxide detectors installed near sleeping areas and checked regularly?

- Are fire extinguishers easily accessible, and does everyone in the house know how to use them?
- Are windows on the second level or higher secure and locked to prevent falls?

6. Emergency preparedness:

- Is a first-aid kit readily available and stocked with essential supplies?
- Have emergency contact numbers, including poison control and pediatrician, been saved in your phone?
- Do you have an evacuation plan in case of fire or other emergencies?

Bonus tips:

- Anchor heavy furniture to the wall using furniture straps.
- Use corner protectors on sharp furniture edges to prevent injuries.
- Install safety gates at both the top and bottom of stairs to avoid falls.

By completing this checklist and taking the necessary precautions, you're creating a safe environment for your little one to explore and grow. Keep up the good work, and remember, safety first!

You've made it through the essential crash course on keeping your little one safe and sound. Remember, it's not about wrapping your child in bubble wrap (although sometimes it feels like it!), but rather creating a safe environment where they can explore and grow without unnecessary risks.

Now, it's time to roll up your sleeves and put those safety measures into action. Take a walk around your home with fresh eyes, looking for any potential dangers lurking in corners or atop shelves. Get down on your hands and knees to see the world from your child's perspective. Review your childproofing every six months as your child grows.

In the next chapter, we'll shift gears from safety to fun and learning. We'll explore how play is not just a way to pass the time but a vital tool for your child's development. Get ready to dive into the exciting world of playtime and discover how you, as a dad, can be a superhero in your child's eyes as they explore, learn, and grow.

CHAPTER 7
INSPIRING THROUGH PLAY

Welcome to the seventh stage of the D.A.D.S. G.U.I.D.E. Framework. Did you know that children learn more in their first three years than they will ever learn again in their lifetime (*Toddler Development and Milestones*, 2023)? It's time to put on your play hat because we're exploring the world of playtime with a purpose. As a new dad, you might think play is just about keeping your little one entertained, but it's so much more than that. In this chapter, we're going to unlock the power of play in shaping your child's educational and ethical development.

From stacking blocks to pretending to be pirates on a living room adventure, every play session is an opportunity for your child to learn and grow. By the end of this chapter, you'll have a treasure trove of creative ideas for play that not only spark joy but also promote learning.

CREATIVE PLAY IDEAS

This is all about building those essential bonds and laying down some serious brainpower foundations. Here's a handy guide for play activities that'll tickle your child's fancy and nurture their growing minds at every stage (*5 Types of Developmental*, 2023):

Newborn stage (0–3 months):

- **Sensory stimulation:** Your baby is like a sponge soaking in everything around them. Introduce them to various textures like soft fabrics, crinkly paper, or smooth toys. You'll see those little eyes light up with curiosity.
- **Gentle sounds:** Soft music or gentle lullabies can soothe your baby while also stimulating their auditory senses. Try singing or humming to them during cuddle time.

Infant stage (4–6 months):

- **Tummy time adventures:** Get down on the floor with your baby during tummy time. Encourage reaching for colorful toys or rattles, which helps strengthen their neck muscles and coordination.
- **Peek-a-boo:** It's a classic for a reason! Cover your face with your hands or a blanket, and then reveal yourself with a big smile. This simple game boosts their cognitive development and brings on those infectious baby giggles.

Budding explorer (7–12 months):

- **Exploration station:** Set up a safe space with different objects for your little explorer to touch, bang, and shake. Think of safe household items like plastic containers, wooden spoons, or soft balls. Let their curiosity run wild!
- **Book bonanza:** Introduce sturdy board books with colorful pictures and simple words. Reading together not only fosters a love for books but also enhances language development.

Toddler time (1–3 years):

- **Messy play:** Embrace the mess with activities like finger painting, water play, or playing with sensory bins filled with rice or pasta. It's all about exploring different textures and sensations.
- **Role-playing:** Break out the dress-up clothes and let your toddler's imagination soar. Whether they want to be a doctor, a chef, or a superhero, role-playing encourages creativity and social skills.

Preschool prodigy (3+ years):

- **Building blocks:** Invest in a set of building blocks or Legos. Not only are they fun, but they also help with fine motor skills, spatial awareness, and problem-solving.
- **Nature walks:** Take your little one on outdoor adventures to explore nature. Point out birds, bugs, flowers, and trees, sparking their curiosity about the world around them.

Remember, the best play activities are the ones where you both have fun and make memories together. Keep it light, keep it engaging, and watch your bond with your little one grow stronger with each playful moment.

One Dad's Story of Finding a Unique Way to Make Memories

Frank, a dad with a hunger for books, passed on his bookworm genes to his daughter, Anna. When he wasn't working, Frank tried to find creative ways to spend time with his children.

Driven by his desire to give his daughter the world, Frank decided to show Anna the enchanting realm of the library. At just six years old, Anna proudly obtained her first library card, kickstarting their beloved Wednesday night library adventures!

Like clockwork, every Wednesday night, Frank and Anna embarked on their library adventure. Anna, with the enthusiasm of a puppy chasing a ball, would scour the shelves for books, while Frank, the patient storyteller, would bring the words to life for her. Among all their library escapades, one memory shines the brightest in Anna's mind: the moment she laid eyes on a paperback featuring a majestic unicorn on its lime green cover, drawn with a bright yellow pencil.

That book didn't just capture her heart; it turned her into a book-devouring bookworm for life!

PREPARATION FOR EARLY SCHOOLING

Now, I know it sounds a bit early to think about school when your baby's still tiny, but it's never too soon to start laying the groundwork.

Playtime isn't just about having fun (although that's definitely a big part of it!). It's also a crucial way for your child to learn and grow. When they're playing, they're actually building all sorts of skills to help them succeed in school and beyond.

When your little tyke is playing, they're not only flexing their muscles and getting those wiggles out (which is great for their physical health), but they're also sharpening their minds. Yup, that's right, playtime helps boost their brainpower and strengthens their cognitive health, making them sharper and more ready to tackle new challenges.

Play also teaches them how to interact with others. Whether playing with you, their siblings, or other kids at daycare, they learn important social skills like sharing, taking turns, and getting along with others. And let's not forget about independence. When they're playing, they're figuring out how to entertain themselves and solve problems on their own, which is a crucial skill for school success.

So, bottom line: Don't underestimate the power of play. It's not just about fun and games; it's about setting your child up for success in school and beyond.

Advice From Early Childhood Educators

What do the experts say? They want to remind you that this is a big milestone, but let's keep our cool. Making a huge fuss might actually stress out your kid more than excite them. Here's the lowdown on how to keep things light and fun:

- **Role-playing:** Get into some pretend play action. Take turns being the parent, the child, and even the teacher. Act out daily routines like saying bye-bye to Mom or Dad, taking off coats, singing songs, and having circle time. Reassure your child that preschool is all about fun and learning. Answer their questions patiently—it helps them feel more in charge and less anxious.
- **Story time:** Hit the books! Head to your local library and grab some reads about preschool adventures. Dive into the stories with your little one and chat about how the characters are feeling. Don't forget to ask your kids how they're feeling, too.
- **Skills practice:** Turn self-help skills into games. Practice unzipping coats, hanging them up, putting on backpacks, and fastening shoes. Have a shoe-tying race or pack a lunch together for a pretend picnic. It's all about getting those skills down pat before the big day.
- **Field trip:** Take a tour of the new preschool together. Hang out on the playground a few times before the real deal starts. Familiarity breeds confidence, so these visits will help ease any nerves.

Now, onto those worries and watching out for signs of stress:

- **Listen up:** When your child shares their worries, don't brush them off. Let them know you hear them loud and clear. Starting something new can be nerve-wracking, so validate their feelings. Share a story of your own new beginnings to show them they're not alone. And hey, if they're worried about missing you, whip up a family photo book to keep in their cubby for comfort.
- **Read the signs:** Sometimes, the little ones can't quite put their worries into words. Keep an eye out for nonverbal cues like clinginess, withdrawal, or even regression in other areas like potty training. It's all part of the adjustment process. Be patient and supportive—this transition is a big deal for them, and they might need some extra love from you.

INSTILLING VALUES AND ETHICS

I would like to take a moment to discuss how you can instill some solid values and ethics into your little one, all while having fun together. Playtime can be a great time for teaching your child important life lessons. Here's how:

- **Labeled feelings:** Start by teaching your child about emotions. You can use simple games to help them recognize and label different feelings. For example, play a game where you both make faces expressing different emotions and then talk about what those emotions mean.

- **Photo books:** Create photo books together featuring family members, friends, and different cultures. Use these books to spark conversations about diversity, inclusion, and empathy.
- **Board games:** Board games are fantastic for teaching communication skills, teamwork, and fair play. Choose games that require cooperation and strategizing, and make sure to discuss the importance of following rules and taking turns.
- **Acts of kindness:** Encourage your child to perform small acts of kindness, like helping a friend or sharing toys. You can even have them start in the home by helping mom with dinner or taking a neighbor some flowers. Acknowledge and praise these actions to reinforce the value of kindness.
- **The golden rule:** Teach your child the golden rule—treat others as you would like to be treated. Use everyday situations to illustrate this principle, like taking turns on the playground or sharing snacks.
- **Modeling helpfulness:** Be a role model for your child by demonstrating helpful behavior yourself. Let them see you lending a hand to others and explaining why it's important to support one another.
- **Role play:** Role-playing scenarios can help your child understand different perspectives and practice conflict resolution. Act out situations like sharing toys or resolving disagreements with siblings to teach problem-solving skills.
- **Differences and similarities:** Use stories or games to celebrate differences and find common ground with others. Help your child understand that diversity enriches our lives and that we should embrace everyone, regardless of their differences.

- **Stories and movies:** Choose books and movies with moral lessons that align with your values. After reading or watching, discuss the story together and ask questions to encourage critical thinking.
- **Feelings and emotions:** Encourage your child to express their feelings openly and listen attentively when they do. Validate their emotions and teach them healthy ways to manage and communicate their feelings.
- **Paper chain of kindness:** Create a paper chain where each link represents an act of kindness. Add a link to the chain whenever your child does something kind, and watch the chain grow as a visual reminder of the positive impact they can have on others.
- **Stand in my shoes:** Help your child understand empathy by encouraging them to imagine how others might feel in different situations. Ask questions like, "How would you feel if someone took your toy without asking?"
- **Kindness to animals:** Teach your child compassion toward animals by caring for pets or observing wildlife together. Talk about the importance of treating animals with kindness and respect.
- **Kindness calendar:** Create a kindness calendar with daily acts of kindness for your child to complete. These can be simple gestures like saying thank you, complimenting someone, or helping with chores around the house.
- **Social awareness:** Engage your child in discussions about social issues and encourage them to think critically about the world around them. Help them understand their role in creating positive change and standing up for what is right.

Remember, the key is to make learning about values and ethics enjoyable and relatable for your child. By incorporating these activities into your playtime together, you'll be laying a solid foundation for their development as compassionate and responsible individuals. Keep it fun and keep it engaging.

INTERACTIVE ELEMENT: PARENT–CHILD PLAY JOURNAL

This is a place for you to record and reflect on play sessions. It can be a valuable tool for tracking developmental progress and memorable moments. This journal isn't just about scribbling down notes; it's a tool for bonding, learning, and creating lasting memories with your little one.

Section 1: Playtime Adventures

- **Date:**_____
- **Activity:** Describe the play activity you engaged in with your child.

How did my child respond?: Jot down your observations on how your child reacted during the play session.

What did we both learn?: Reflect on any new skills, discoveries, or insights gained during play.

Section 2: Memorable Moments

- **Date:**_____
- **Activity:** Describe the play activity or special moment you shared with your child.

Why was it memorable? Share what made this moment stand out and why it's worth remembering.

Reflection: Take a moment to reflect on the significance of this moment for both you and your child.

Section 3: Developmental Milestones

- **Date:** _____
- **Observations:** Note any developmental milestones or progress you noticed during playtime.

>

Areas for growth: Identify any areas where your child might need a little extra encouragement or support.

>

Plans for next time: Outline your ideas for future play sessions to support your child's development.

>

Section 4: Playtime Goals

Short-term goals: List some achievable goals you have for your playtime with your child in the next week or so.

>

Long-term goals: Think about the kind of relationship you want to build with your child through play and jot down some long-term goals.

Reflection: Reflect on how achieving these goals will benefit both you and your child.

Throughout this chapter, we have talked about the importance of play in your child's development and how it fosters learning, creativity, and bonding. From peek-a-boo to building block towers, every interaction with your little one is an opportunity for growth and connection.

Now, it's time to put these ideas into action. Get down on the floor, roll up your sleeves, and dive into the world of play with your child. Embrace the mess, the giggles, and the endless imagination that comes with it.

In the next chapter, we'll take a deeper dive into maintaining a harmonious family life, nurturing your child's social skills, and finding balance in all aspects of fatherhood. Get ready to explore how to create a supportive environment where your child can thrive.

CHAPTER 8
DEVELOPING FAMILY HARMONY AND SOCIAL WELL-BEING

We are moving on to the eighth stage of the D.A.D.S. G.U.I.D.E. Framework. How does your well-being as a father directly impact your child's mental and physical health, and what steps can you take to improve it?

Welcome to the family harmony boot camp, where we're diving deep into the dynamics of creating a happy, healthy environment for you, your partner, and your little one. I get it; life feels like a whirlwind right now. Between the doctor's appointments and the teething, the last thing you might think about is family harmony. But carving out time for this is like investing in the future happiness of your entire bunch.

In this chapter, we're not just talking about keeping the peace at home (although that's definitely part of it). We're also delving into how your family's social well-being plays a crucial role in your child's development and your own.

FAMILY PHYSICAL AND MENTAL WELLNESS

It's time to talk about the importance of maintaining the entire team's well-being—both physically and mentally. Everyone, including yourself, your partner, and the lovable little ones, must prioritize their health.

First, let's get moving! When we're all more active together, it's like hitting the jackpot of health benefits. We're talking about maintaining a healthy weight, kicking stress to the curb, and lowering the risk of serious stuff like heart disease. Plus, it's a blast! You can make it happen, rain or shine. Consider a stroll around the block, ditching the elevator for the stairs, or getting creative indoors. And hey, making it a family affair not only keeps everyone motivated but also creates some killer hobbies that'll stick around for the long haul.

Now, about getting everyone in on the action–it's game time! Round up the troops and brainstorm activities together. Why not try post-dinner walks, splashing around in the pool, or even tackling chores as a team? The key is keeping everyone engaged and having fun. And the options? Endless! From indoor rock climbing to roller skating rinks, there's something for everyone.

It is important to lead by example. Show your crew what it means to prioritize health by lacing up those sneakers and hitting the pavement. Offer a hand when needed, cheer on those little victories, and let them know their efforts are gold. It's all about creating a positive environment where healthy choices are celebrated.

Getting active together isn't just about staying fit; it's about strengthening those family ties. Whether it's cheering on your kiddo's soccer team or tackling a new hobby together, these moments are the ones you'll cherish forever. So, grab your gear, rally the troops, and let's make some memories while staying fit as a fiddle.

Tips on Fostering Mental Wellness and Stress Management for Both Parents and Children

Here are some down-to-earth tips on nurturing mental wellness and handling stress for both you and your little one:

- Be real about what you expect. Don't set the bar too high for yourself or your partner. Babies don't come with instruction manuals, so cut yourself some slack.

- Build up a solid support crew. Whether it's family, friends, or other parents, having folks you can lean on and swap war stories with is invaluable.
- Remember, you're not just a dad; you're a person, too. Take time for yourself, even if it's just a quick breather to grab a coffee or go for a walk. You'll come back refreshed and ready to tackle those diaper changes like a pro.
- Exercise isn't just for shedding that dad bod—it's also a killer stress-buster. Even if it's just a few push-ups during nap time or a stroll around the block with the stroller, getting moving can work wonders for your mental state.
- Cut yourself some slack. You're not going to be perfect, and that's okay. Babies cry, diapers leak, and sleep is a luxury. Roll with the punches and give yourself credit for just showing up.
- Tough times don't last forever. Remember that phase where your little one refuses to sleep longer than 20 minutes at a time? It'll pass, eventually.
- Don't be afraid to reach out for help. Whether chatting with friends, seeking advice from family, or talking to a pro, getting things off your chest can be a game-changer.
- Trust your gut. You know your baby better than anyone else, so don't second-guess yourself.
- Be mindful of how other people's opinions and actions can affect your mood. Sometimes, it's best to tune out the peanut gallery and do what feels right for your family.
- Quit playing the comparison game. Every baby is different, and every family has its own quirks. Focus on what works for you, not what the Joneses are doing.
- Skip the booze and drugs as stress relievers. Trust me, the hangover with a crying baby is no fun, and dependency is no laughing matter.

- Have a plan for when things get overwhelming, whether it's calling in reinforcements or taking a breather in another room, and know when to hit the pause button.
- Pay attention to how long you've been feeling stressed. It's normal to have rough patches, but if you're constantly on edge, it might be time to seek some extra support.

ENCOURAGING SOCIAL SKILLS AND FRIENDSHIPS

Every parent wants their child to make friends and feel comfortable in social situations. It might seem premature, but knowing how to help your little human develop and nurture these skills early is beneficial. Here's what you can do:

- **Model social behavior:** Your child is always watching how you react and what you do in situations. Show them how to interact by being a good role model yourself. Be polite, kind, and respectful in your interactions with others, whether with your partner, friends, or strangers.
- **Encourage playdates:** Start them young! Arrange playdates with other kids their age. It's not just for the kids; it's an excellent opportunity for you to bond with other fathers, too.
- **Practice empathy:** Help your child understand other people's feelings by talking about emotions. When they see someone sad, explain why they might feel that way. Reading books about feelings can also be a great way to teach empathy.
- **Foster independence:** Let your little one explore and interact with their peers independently. Of course, keep an eye on them, but try not to intervene unless necessary. It

helps them develop confidence and problem-solving skills, essential for navigating social situations.
- **Set playful boundaries:** Socializing also means learning boundaries. Teach your child to respect others' personal space and belongings. It's an important skill that'll serve them well in friendships and beyond.
- **Be patient:** Social skills take time. Your child might stumble along the way, and that's okay. Offer guidance, support, and lots of encouragement. Every little step counts.

Tips on Organizing Playdates and Encouraging Friendships

Here's what you need to know: Connecting your little one with their peers is like giving them a head start to becoming a mini social butterfly. Here are some tips to make it smooth sailing:

- **Connect and follow through:** Don't just talk about setting up playdates; actually do it. Be proactive and follow through. Your kid's social life doesn't just happen on its own.
- **Schedule playdates wisely:** Don't overwhelm yourself or your kid with too many playdates in one go. Spread them out so they're enjoyable for everyone involved. Be mindful of schedules and time. Scheduling a playdate right after soccer practice and before dinner could be a recipe for disaster.
- **Set a playdate endpoint:** Having a clear finish line can save you from endless meltdowns. Set a time limit so your child doesn't burn out and they are prepared for pick up times.

- **Plan your playdate on neutral ground:** Pick a spot that is fair game for both kids. It takes the pressure off and makes things feel more equal. Rather than always being at one child's house or the other, choose a park or the library.
- **Consider a low-key playdate activity:** You don't need to plan a full-on extravaganza. Keep it simple with activities like coloring, building blocks, or just running around in the park.
- **Bring a little something to your playdate:** A snack or a toy can be a nice gesture. It's like a mini icebreaker for the kids. I would recommend this if it is your child's first time meeting with this child, but it isn't necessary on every visit.
- **Handle playdate hiccups calmly:** Tantrums, disagreements; you name it—they might happen. Stay cool, calm, and collected. It's all part of the playdate journey. Your job is to be impartial.
- **Keep the playdate momentum going:** Once you've got the ball rolling, don't let it drop. Stay in touch with other parents and keep those playdates coming.
- **Don't give up:** Sometimes, it takes a bit of trial and error to find the perfect playdate groove. Don't throw in the towel if things don't click right away. Keep at it, and before you know it, your kid will be the talk of the sandbox.

BALANCING WORK AND FATHERHOOD

Are you losing sleep at night, wondering about the balance between work and fatherhood? This is a common problem for all fathers. In fact, 52% of dads find it hard to balance work and family life (Taylor, 2022). Here are some practical strategies to help you keep all the balls in the air:

- **Family calendar:** Wrangle the chaos by setting up a family calendar. Sync it with your partner to keep track of appointments, important dates, and who's on baby duty and when.
- **Childcare champions:** Secure reliable childcare and build a solid relationship with your caregiver. Trust is key here, so communicate openly and regularly about your child's needs and routines.
- **Separate and dominate:** Teamwork makes everything easier. Divide responsibilities with your partner to share the load fairly. You are in this together, so support one another and communicate about the tasks that need to be completed.
- **Emergency babysitter plan:** Always have a backup babysitter on standby. Emergencies happen, and having a reliable backup will save you from scrambling at the last minute.
- **Streamlined mornings:** Make mornings as smooth as possible by prepping the night before. Lay out clothes, pack bags, and have breakfast essentials ready to go. It'll save you time and stress.
- **Workplace support:** Don't be afraid to ask for support at work. Whether it's flexible hours, remote work options, or understanding colleagues, having a supportive workplace can make a world of difference.
- **Bedtime routine brilliance:** Establish a soothing bedtime routine to help your little one wind down. Consistency is key here, so stick to the same rituals every night to signal that it's time to sleep. Don't forget to do the same for yourself!

- **Dinner simplified:** Keep dinner simple and stress-free with easy meal prep and quick recipes. Embrace the wonders of one-pot meals and takeout when needed. Your sanity is worth it.
- **Self-care corner:** Remember to take care of yourself. Schedule some "me time" to recharge your batteries. Hit the gym, read a book, or indulge in a hobby.
- **Networking necessity:** Maintain a network of supportive contacts, both in and out of the workplace. Having a circle of fellow dads and friends who understand your struggles can provide invaluable support and camaraderie.
- **Mastering the art of "no":** Learn to say no when your plate is already full. Prioritize what's truly important, and don't overcommit yourself. Your time and energy are precious commodities.
- **Stay laser-focused:** When you're at work, give it your all. Stay focused, be productive, and tackle tasks efficiently so you can leave on time and be fully present for your family.
- **Snuggle sessions:** Sneak in some quality snuggle time with your little one whenever you can. Those cuddles are not just for them—they're also therapeutic for you, helping to melt away stress and strengthen your bond.

Real-Life Stories of Dads Who Have Found Balance

Meet Joe, who dove into fatherhood while navigating law school. Balancing time became imperative. Joe suggests finding a routine that suits you and sharing your calendar with your partner. Teamwork was what saved him and helped him find those precious moments with his family.

And let's not forget Mark, the CEO extraordinaire. Mark makes it a point to leave work early every Monday to coach his twin sons' hockey team. He firmly believes that putting family first actually boosts work performance. He finds this gives him bonus time with his children and is a great stress reliever at the same time.

Bob is in an executive leadership role and stresses the importance of establishing a clear line between his professional and personal life. His consistent job performance gives him the freedom to prioritize taking calls from his kids over business calls and scheduling key business meetings around his children's academic calendar. To sum up, Bob says fathers need to make intentional decisions around work-life balance and consistently follow through on them.

INTERACTIVE ELEMENT: FAMILY WELLNESS PLAN

Now that you've got this amazing new addition to your family, it's important to make sure everyone stays healthy and happy. That's where a family wellness plan comes in. This will help you set goals for physical activities, meals, and mental health practices for you, your partner, and your little one. Let's get started!

Physical activities:

- **Goal:** How many days per week do you want to engage in physical activities as a family?

- **Activities:** What kind of activities do you enjoy doing together? (e.g., walking, playing at the park, swimming)

- **Duration:** How long do you aim to spend on each activity session?

Meals:

- **Goal:** How many home-cooked meals do you want to aim for each week?

- **Meal planning:** Take some time to plan out your weekly meals. Consider including a variety of fruits, vegetables, lean proteins, and whole grains.

Monday	Tuesday	Wednesday	Thursday	Friday	Saturday	Sunday

- **Cooking together:** Get everyone involved in meal preparation. It's a great way to bond as a family and teach your little one about healthy eating habits.

Mental health practices:

- **Goal:** How often do you want to prioritize mental health practices as a family?

- **Practices:** What mental health practices do you find helpful? (e.g., mindfulness exercises, family discussions, relaxation techniques)

- **Support system:** Which friends, family members, or professionals can you turn to for support when needed?

Remember, the key to success is setting realistic goals and taking small steps toward achieving them. It's okay if things don't always go according to plan; what matters is that you're making an effort to prioritize your family's well-being.

Feel free to adjust your goals as needed and celebrate your achievements along the way. Here's to a happy and healthy journey with your new family!

We've covered a lot in this chapter about building a strong family foundation and fostering harmony within your household. Remember, it's not just about changing diapers and baby-proofing the house but also about cultivating an environment where everyone feels loved, supported, and heard.

Now, it's time to put these ideas into action. Start by having a heart-to-heart with your partner about how you can better support each other and create a harmonious environment for your family. Set some goals, make a plan, and most importantly, enjoy the journey together.

With a strong foundation in family harmony and social well-being, it's time to look toward the future. In the final chapter, we will explore how to cherish and celebrate your family's milestones and prepare for the ongoing journey of growth and change.

CHAPTER 9
ENVISIONING THE FUTURE

Welcome to the ninth and final stage of the D.A.D.S. G.U.I.D.E. Framework. As you watch your child grow, have you considered what kind of legacy you want to leave for them and future generations?

Welcome to the final chapter, which is all about gazing into the crystal ball of fatherhood. In this chapter, we will dive into the horizon of fatherhood, exploring the bigger picture and the legacy you're building with every coo, every giggle, and every bedtime story.

Within these pages, you'll discover how to celebrate those little victories, adapt to the ever-evolving needs of your growing family, and reflect on the profound impact you have on shaping the future, not just for your kids but for generations to come.

CELEBRATING MILESTONES AND MAKING MEMORIES

Welcome to the fun zone, Dad! Today, we're stepping into the world of milestone celebrations, where every achievement deserves a round of applause and maybe even a confetti cannon (just kidding, let's not clean that up).

As dads, we've got front-row seats to the greatest show on earth—watching our little munchkins grow, learn, and conquer the world, one milestone at a time. From their first gummy grin to their triumphant first steps, these moments are what memories are made of.

But why settle for the ordinary when you can sprinkle a little extra magic on those milestone moments? In this section, we're ditching the cookie-cutter celebrations and diving headfirst into a treasure trove of creative ideas to make those milestones shine brighter than a disco ball at a dance party.

So grab your party hats, dust off your dancing shoes, and get ready to unleash your inner kid because we're about to take milestone celebrations to a whole new level. Get ready to create memories that'll make your child's childhood truly unforgettable—one milestone at a time.

- **Creating rituals or traditions:** First, establishing some traditions or rituals can be just what everyone needs. It doesn't have to be fancy or elaborate. It could be as simple as a bedtime story every night or a weekend pancake breakfast. These little routines help build a sense of security and connection for both you and your little one. These can be just what memories are made of.
- **Expressing words of affirmation:** Let's talk about affirmations. Yes, those little words of encouragement can make a big difference. Whether it's a simple "I love you" or praising their efforts, letting your child know they're valued and appreciated can boost their self-esteem and strengthen your bond.
- **Gifting meaningful tokens:** Gifts don't have to break the bank to be meaningful. It could be a handmade card, a favorite book, or even a rock they found on a special outing together. The key is thoughtfulness, not price tag.
- **Reflecting on the journey:** Take a moment to pause and reflect on how far you've come. Parenthood is a wild ride, and celebrating milestones is a great opportunity to look back on the journey so far and appreciate all the little victories along the way.

- **Setting sights on the future:** While it's important to celebrate where you are now, it's also good to look ahead. Talk with your partner about your hopes and dreams for your child's future, and maybe even start some savings or planning for big milestones down the road.
- **Using milestones as teaching moments:** Every milestone is a chance to learn something new. Whether it's learning to tie their shoes or ride a bike, use these moments as opportunities to teach valuable life skills and instill a sense of confidence and independence.
- **Encouraging altruism and gratitude:** Teaching your child to give back and appreciate what they have is a priceless gift. Consider celebrating milestones by volunteering together or starting a gratitude journal to reflect on the good things in life.
- **Tailoring celebrations to your child's interests:** One size does not fit all when it comes to celebrations. Take your child's interests and personality into account when planning special events or activities. Whether they're into dinosaurs or dancing, tailor the celebration to what makes them happy. Keep in mind that not all children love the intensity of huge parties. Don't feel the societal pressure to cave, either. If your toddler is more content with just mom and dad, so be it.
- **Involving them in planning:** Finally, don't forget to involve your child in the planning process. Let them have a say in how they want to celebrate their milestones, whether it's choosing the menu for their birthday dinner or picking out decorations for a special occasion. It's their moment, after all!

- **Take lots of photos:** Alright, let's talk paparazzi mode! Snap away at those milestone moments. Whether it's their first smile or their first spaghetti faceplant, these photos will be priceless memories down the road. And hey, don't worry about being a pro photographer because blurry shots and funny faces add character!
- **Make a video:** Lights, camera, action! Grab your smartphone and capture those milestone moments in motion. From their wobbly first steps to their adorable babbling, a video will let you relive these precious moments whenever you need a pick-me-up.
- **Keep a journal:** Time to channel your inner writer! Start jotting down those milestone moments in a journal. Include not just the milestones, but also your thoughts and feelings. Reading back on these entries will tug at your heartstrings like nothing else.
- **Create a memory box:** Get crafty and create a memory box for your child's keepsakes. Toss in their first pair of shoes, that beloved stuffed animal they can't sleep without, or even little notes from family members. It's like a time capsule of their childhood.
- **Throw a party:** Time to party, party, party! Celebrate those milestones with a bang by throwing a themed bash. Whether it's a superhero shindig or a princess extravaganza, deck out the backyard, invite friends and family, and indulge in some tasty treats. And hey, why not toss in some inflatable fun for good measure? Water slides, bounce houses—you name it, it's a guaranteed hit! Just remember, your wee one should want this.

- **Plan a special outing:** Pack your bags and hit the road! Plan an adventure-filled outing to celebrate those milestones. Maybe a trip to the zoo to see the lions roar or a camping excursion under the stars? These experiences will create lasting memories for both you and your little one. Think outside the box, too, science centers, petting zoos, even amusement parks are fair game.

ADAPTING TO FAMILY'S EVOLVING NEEDS

One thing is inevitable. Your little one is going to grow right before your eyes faster than you can imagine. How can you continue to roll with the punches? Be prepared! Let's review the stages you should expect (*Adapting Your Parenting Style*, 2013):

- **Image-making (pregnancy):** You're gearing up for the big change, imagining how life will look with a mini-me in tow. Get ready to embrace the adventure.
- **Nurturing (birth to 18–24 months):** From the moment your baby arrives, you're learning the delicate dance of meeting their needs while juggling work, your partner, friends, and the household. It's all about finding balance in the chaos.
- **Authoritative (2–5 years):** Now it's time to lay down the law—well, sort of. You're setting boundaries and rules, making sure your little tornado stays safe. But hey, don't forget to explain why those rules exist. It's all about teaching them to make good choices down the road.
- **Interpretive (5–12 years):** Your child's growing up, learning to see the world through other people's eyes. It's not just about playing nice; they're navigating the ups and downs of friendships, dealing with bullies, and finding

their place in the pack. Your job? Helping them move through these social minefields.
- **Interdependent (the adolescence stage):** Brace yourself—teenage turbulence is coming. As your teen starts spreading their wings, tensions might rise. It's crucial to keep those lines of communication wide open, not just with your kid but with your partner, too.
- **Departure (late adolescence to young adulthood):** And just like that, your baby's all grown up (well, almost). As they step into independence, it's time for you to redefine your role too. Sure, there might be a tear or two shed as they fly the nest, but it's also a chance for you to rediscover yourself. Embrace the journey as they embrace theirs.

Insights From the Experts

Experts are calling this generation "the great acceleration." Things are moving fast, creating all sorts of challenges for us as we take on the parenting gig. The result? Our kids these days are facing some serious struggles—anxiety, lack of motivation, you name it. Did you know that more than 40% of high school students showed signs of depression in 2022? Yeah, it's a tough stat to swallow. And even before the chaos of recent times, nearly one in three adolescents had anxiety issues (Tedesco et al., 2023).

We all want to help our kids thrive, right? Unfortunately, the old ways of pushing our kids to be the best might not be cutting it anymore. Instead of obsessing over grades or achievements, we need to focus on something different: adaptability.

Our kids need to be able to roll with the punches, handle tough emotions, and think on their feet. Forget about always having the right answers; it's all about being okay with the "maybe."

So, how do we do it? Well, it starts with a shift in mindset. Instead of constantly swooping in to save the day, sometimes, we need to step back and let our kids figure things out on their own. It's not always easy, but it's important.

We also have to teach them to handle uncertainty with ease. Life's unpredictable, right? Instead of trying to control every little thing, we need to show our kids how to embrace the unknown and move forward with confidence.

And hey, let's not forget about the digital world. Too much screen time can mess with our kids' little brains, so let's encourage some old-school fun—like playing outside or getting creative without a screen in sight.

Parenting is a tough job, no doubt about it. But by focusing on building adaptability in our kids, we're setting them up for success in whatever comes their way.

LEAVING A LASTING LEGACY

When we talk about legacy, we're not just talking about leaving behind a pile of money or a fancy house. We're talking about the stuff that really matters—the emotional, social, and spiritual bits that shape who our kids become and how they interact with the world.

The Emotional Legacy

Think of your family as the soil where emotional roots grow. It's your job to create an environment where those roots can dig deep and strong. Here's how:

- **Safety and stability:** Be the rock that your family can lean on. Consistency and reliability go a long way in building confidence.
- **Trusting support:** Show your kids that you've got their backs, no matter what. Let them know they can come to you with anything.
- **Positive identity:** Help your kids see the best in themselves. Give them space to explore who they are and celebrate their uniqueness.
- **Soul sanctuary:** Your home should be more than just a place to crash. It should be a refuge—a place where your family feels safe and at peace.
- **Unconditional love:** Love them when they're adorable little angels and when they're driving you up the wall. They need to know that your love is not going anywhere.

The Social Legacy

Teach your kids how to navigate the world with grace and respect:

- **Respect:** Start at home by showing respect to each other. Then, extend that respect to everyone you meet.
- **Responsibility:** Give your kids chores and tasks to do around the house. It teaches them that actions have consequences and helps them grow into responsible adults.

- **Boundaries:** Set clear boundaries for how your family interacts with others. Whether it's with friends, authority figures, or the environment, make sure your kids know where the lines are.

The Spiritual Legacy

You don't have to be religious to pass down important spiritual values:

- **Personal connection:** Help your kids see that there's something bigger than themselves out there. It might be God, nature, or just the power of love, showing them that there's more to life than what meets the eye.
- **Routine and rituals:** Make spiritual activities a regular part of your family life. Whether it's saying grace before meals or taking a moment for quiet reflection, these little rituals can have a big impact.
- **Timeless truth:** Talk to your kids about the things that really matter—love, kindness, forgiveness. Help them understand that these principles are timeless and universal.
- **Everyday spirituality:** Show your kids that spirituality is not just for special occasions. It's something that can be woven into the fabric of everyday life, from how we treat others to how we make decisions.

LIFE LESSONS FROM A FATHER

Get ready for some priceless life lessons that only a dad can share. These are the teachings that will stick with our little ones forever!

- **Volunteer as a family:** Alright, so volunteering is not just about lending a hand. It's about showing empathy, compassion, and responsibility in action. When you roll up your sleeves together, you're not just helping out; you're teaching your kids values that'll stay with them forever. Try serving meals at a shelter or cleaning up the neighborhood park. Show your children how to make a difference while teaching important life lessons.
- **Start a family charity project:** Now, this might sound fancy, but it's all about putting your passions to good use. Whether you're into education, the environment, or something else entirely, you can start a project as a family. Maybe it's organizing fundraisers or teaming up with local groups. Whatever it is, you're showing your kids that you can make a real impact by working together on something meaningful.
- **Be smart with your money:** Alright, forget about big money moves! It's the small stuff that really counts. Managing money is like a slow dance, not a flashy show. Be modest and smart with your money.
- **Live within your means:** Here's the deal—living with less can actually make you richer. Seriously. When you're not constantly chasing after more stuff, you've got more control over your life. It's not about how much you make; it's about how much you need to be happy.

- **It's okay to pivot:** Life's a journey, and sometimes you end up on a different path than you planned. And you know what? That's okay. Changing your mind is a power move, not a weakness. So don't be afraid to pivot when you need to.
- **Decide what is worth your time and money:** Everything has a price. Whether it's time, relationships, or creativity, everything comes with a cost. It's up to you to decide what's worth paying for.
- **Be kind:** Look, money's nice and all, but it's not the measure of true success. What really matters is how you treat people. Building genuine connections is worth more than any bank account.

INTERACTIVE ELEMENT: A LETTER TO MY FUTURE CHILD (A TEMPLATE)

Dear [Child's Name],

As I sit down to write this letter to you, I can't help but feel a flood of emotions. You're not even here yet, but I already feel like I know you in some inexplicable way. Maybe it's the countless nights your mom and I spent imagining what you'd be like or the palpable excitement that fills our home as we prepare for your arrival. Whatever it is, know that you are already deeply loved, cherished, and anticipated.

- **Introduce yourself:** Hi there, little one! It's your dad writing to you from the past, eagerly awaiting the day I get to hold you in my arms.

- **Hopes and dreams:** I hope for so many things for you. I hope you find happiness in the little moments, courage in the face of challenges, and kindness in your heart always. I dream of watching you grow and discover the world, of seeing your eyes light up with wonder as you experience life's adventures.
- **Advice:** Listen, kiddo, life's going to get messy, but always remember to stay true to yourself. Don't be afraid to chase your dreams, even if they seem out of reach. And never underestimate the power of a good laugh: It can work wonders, even on the toughest days.
- **Expressions of love:** I want you to know, without a shadow of a doubt, that you are loved beyond measure. From the moment we knew you were coming into our lives, you became our greatest joy, our most cherished treasure. And that love will only grow with each passing day.
- **Closing words:** Well, little one, I'll wrap up this letter for now, but know that I'll be eagerly counting down the days until I can finally hold you in my arms and tell you all these things in person. Until then, know that you are always in my thoughts and in my heart.

With all my love,

Your Dad

Feel free to add your personal touch, anecdotes, or anything else that comes to mind. This letter is your chance to speak from the heart and let your future child know just how much they mean to you.

As we wrap up this chapter on envisioning the future, let's take a moment to appreciate the wild ride of fatherhood. It's a journey packed with growth spurts, unexpected challenges, and rewards that are priceless. In this guide, you've explored baby wrangling and juggling work and family while discovering fatherhood. As rookie dads, you've soaked up loads of handy tips and wisdom, getting all set for the path ahead!

As you stand at the threshold of this new phase in your life, carry forward the lessons learned and the bonds forged. Continue to prioritize self-care, maintaining a healthy balance between your personal aspirations and your family's needs. Nurture your relationship with your partner, communicate openly, and support each other through the highs and lows of parenthood.

CONCLUSION

You've made it to the end of this guide! Hopefully, you're feeling a bit more confident about this whole fatherhood thing. The goal of this guide is to leave you feeling more prepared, better educated, and ready to tackle the challenges ahead.

From the moment you find out the news that fatherhood is entering your life, it is normal to feel anxious, worried, and downright terrified. Questions begin to keep dads up at night, wondering how they are going to provide, support their partner, and be responsible for an entire tiny human... all while trying to remember where they left their socks!

Be mindful that this resource is like a trusty sidekick, always there for you. As your baby sprouts up like a little beanstalk and your family's whims evolve, dive back in and revisit those sections that tickle your fancy once more!

CONCLUSION

Remember, being a dad is a journey filled with ups and downs, but one thing remains constant: you are an essential part of your child's life.

Throughout this book, we've explored fatherhood using the D.A.D.S. G.U.I.D.E. framework:

- **Discovering fatherhood:** Embrace the emotional journey of becoming a dad. Understand that it's normal to feel overwhelmed and unsure at times, but know that you're not alone in this experience.
- **Attending to bonding:** Forge deep emotional connections with your baby from the very beginning. Spend quality time together, engage in skin-to-skin contact, and participate in caregiving activities to strengthen your bond.
- **Diapering and care:** Learn the practical skills of infant care, from changing diapers to feeding and ensuring proper hygiene. These everyday tasks may seem daunting at first, but with practice, you'll become a pro in no time.
- **Supporting growth and development:** Play an active role in your baby's physical, cognitive, and emotional development. Engage in stimulating activities, read to your child, and provide plenty of love and encouragement along the way.
- **Growing relationships and overcoming challenges:** Nurture your relationships with your partner, your baby, and extended family members. Communication, patience, and understanding are key to overcoming challenges and building strong, lasting connections.

- **Upholding safety:** Create a safe and loving environment for your family at home. Childproof your space, stay informed about safety guidelines, and always prioritize your child's well-being above all else.
- **Inspiring through play:** Encourage learning and development through play and interaction. Get down on the floor, unleash your inner child, and embrace the joy and wonder of discovery alongside your little one.
- **Developing family harmony and social well-being:** Strike a balance between family life, social engagements, and work commitments. Prioritize quality time with your loved ones, set boundaries when necessary, and remember to take care of yourself, too.
- **Envisioning the future:** Look ahead to the future and the ongoing journey of fatherhood. Embrace the challenges and joys that lie ahead, knowing that each moment spent with your child is a precious gift.

After closing this book, you can feel prepared, find work–life balance, maintain strong relationships, and safeguard your mental health. It's all within your reach. Remember, you can revisit any section of this guide as a refresher at any time!

As you embark on this new phase of your life, remember that you're not alone. Countless dads have walked this path before you, facing similar challenges and celebrating similar triumphs.

Take inspiration from those who have thrived in their roles as fathers. Now, it's your turn to create your success story.

Your journey as a dad doesn't stop here! Share the wisdom you've picked up, the challenges you've tackled, and the joys you've savored. Inspire your fellow fathers with your tales! And hey, be ready to soak up the inspiration and wisdom that flows from the hilarious and heartwarming stories of awesome dad squads!

And before you go, if you found this guide helpful, I'd greatly appreciate it if you could leave a review. Your feedback helps get this book into the hands of those new dads who need it most.

Here's to you, your family, and the incredible adventure that lies ahead. Happy fathering!

Keeping the Game Alive

Now that you've got the tools you need to succeed as a new dad, it's your turn to pass on the torch. By sharing your honest thoughts about this book on Amazon, you'll guide other new dads to the support they need and keep the spirit of helpful fatherhood thriving.

Thank you for joining in on this journey. Your experiences and insights are what make fatherhood vibrant and alive when we share what we've learned—and you're a key part of helping us do just that. Your journey matters to us.

Scan the QR code below to leave your review on Amazon:

Your input supports other dads and keeps the community of new fathers informed and connected.

We appreciate your help in making fatherhood a little easier for everyone!

REFERENCES

Adapting your parenting style for your child's developmental stage. (2013, February 9). Melbourne Child Psychology. https://melbournechildpsychology.com.au/blog/adapting-your-parenting-style-for-your-childs-developmental-stage/

Ansong-Assoku, B., & Ankola, P. A. (2023, February 20). *Neonatal jaundice.* Nih.gov; StatPearls Publishing. https://www.ncbi.nlm.nih.gov/books/NBK532930/

Baldovinos, D. (2023, July 24). *How to choose the best diapers for your baby.* Motherhood Center. https://www.motherhoodcenter.com/how-to-choose-the-best-diapers/

Bishop, M. (2023, November 1). *Creating a happy home environment.* Warrenton & Linton Hall Pediatrics. https://warrentonpediatrics.com/creating-a-happy-home-environment/#:

Brennan, D. (2021, March 9). *What age do babies have object permanence?* WebMD. https://www.webmd.com/baby/what-age-do-babies-have-object-permanence

Care.com Editorial Staff. (2021, June 10). *This is how much child care costs in 2021.* Care.com Resources. https://www.care.com/c/how-much-does-child-care-cost/

Caring for a baby with colic (and yourself). (n.d.). Dads Adventure. https://dadsadventure.com/caring-for-a-baby-with-colic-and-yourself/

Centers for Disease Control and Prevention. (2023, March 8). *Data and statistics - SIDS.* Centers for Disease Control and Prevention. https://www.cdc.gov/sids/data.htm

Christiano, D. (2023, February 7). *How can you get your baby on a feeding schedule?* Healthline. https://www.healthline.com/health/parenting/baby-feeding-schedule#schedule-by-age

Connecting with your baby's emotions. (n.d.). First Things First. https://www.firstthingsfirst.org/first-things/connecting-with-your-babys-emotions/

The daddy factor: How fathers support development. (n.d.). ZERO to THREE. https://www.zerotothree.org/resource/the-daddy-factor-how-fathers-support-development/#:

The evolution of emotions (part 1): Your baby's first year. (2017, October 17). Baby Sparks. https://babysparks.com/2017/10/12/the-evolution-of-emotions-part-1-your-babys-first-year/

5 types of developmental activities for children. (2023, June 15). Holly Springs Pediatrics. https://www.myhspediatrics.com/developmental-activities-for-children/

REFERENCES

Gardner, A. (2010, July 26). *Can a mother's affection prevent anxiety in adulthood?* CNN. https://www.cnn.com/2010/HEALTH/07/26/mother.affection.anxiety/

Guntreddi, G. (2017, September 15). *Reading the signs: Decoding your baby's cues.* Sanford Health News. https://news.sanfordhealth.org/childrens/reading-the-signs-decoding-your-babys-cues/

The Headsup Guys Team. (2021, January 31). *Becoming a dad and maintaining your mental health.* HeadsUpGuys. https://headsupguys.org/new-dad-mental-health/

Iannelli, V. (2022, November 27). *Step-by-Step guide to childproofing your home.* Verywell Family. https://www.verywellfamily.com/childproofing-your-home-2634228

Lock, H. (2021, May 21). *270,000 children die at home every year. Meet the doctor trying to change that.* Global Citizen. https://www.globalcitizen.org/en/content/prevent-injury-at-home-child-mortality-uk-aid/

Mauskopf, S. (2023). *8 things new dads really think about new dad life. Winnie.* https://winnie.com/resources/8-things-new-dads-really-think

Mayo Clinic Staff. (2021, June 24). *Common cold in babies - Diagnosis and treatment.* Mayoclinic. https://www.mayoclinic.org/diseases-conditions/common-cold-in-babies/diagnosis-treatment/drc-20351657

McTigue, S. (2020, March 27). *Preparing for fatherhood: 16 ways to get ready.* Healthline. https://www.healthline.com/health/preparing-for-fatherhood

Miller, C. (2016, February 25). *How to handle tantrums and meltdowns.* Child Mind Institute. https://childmind.org/article/how-to-handle-tantrums-and-meltdowns/

Morin, A. (2022). *Developmental milestones from birth to age 1.* Understood. https://www.understood.org/en/articles/developmental-milestones-from-birth-to-age-1

Newborns: Health & daily care. (n.d.). Raising Children Network. https://raisingchildren.net.au/newborns/health-daily-care

Newborn illness - how to recognize. (2023, October 11). Seattle Children's Hospital. https://www.seattlechildrens.org/conditions/a-z/newborn-illness-how-to-recognize/

New dads' guide to play & development for 0-12 months. (2020, August 19). The Dad Tab. https://dadtab.com/new-dads-guide-play-development-baby-0-12-months/

NHS. (2021, December 8). *Helping your baby to sleep.* Nhs.uk. https://www.nhs.uk/conditions/baby/caring-for-a-newborn/helping-your-baby-to-sleep/

Pacheco, D. (2023, April 26). *Infant sleep cycles: How are they different from adults?* Sleep Foundation. https://www.sleepfoundation.org/baby-sleep/baby-sleep-cycle

Patrick. (2023, March 24). *20+ essential self-care tips and activities for dads.* Daddy Simply. https://daddysimply.com/self-care-ideas-for-dads-recharge-and-refresh/

Perry, T. (2024, February 2). *Dad praised for how he handled tantrum.* Upworthy. https://www.upworthy.com/you-set-the-standard-woman-praises-random-dad-for-how-he-handled-toddler-s-target-meltdown

Renter, E. (n.d.). *Would-be parents unprepared for cost of a baby*. NerdWallet. https://www.nerdwallet.com/article/insurance/cost-of-raising-baby#:

Rivelli, E. (2023, March 1). *How much does it cost to have A baby? 2023 averages*. Forbes. https://www.forbes.com/advisor/health-insurance/average-childbirth-cost/#:

Rivero, E. (2013, September 30). *Lack of parental warmth, abuse in childhood linked to multiple health risks in adulthood*. UCLA. https://newsroom.ucla.edu/releases/lack-of-parental-warmth-abuse-248580

Schwartz, S. (2017, November 7). *How a parent's affection shapes a child's happiness for life*. The Gottman Institute. https://www.gottman.com/blog/how-a-parents-affection-shapes-a-childs-happiness-for-life/

Shu, J. (2023, August 14). *Bringing baby home: How to prepare for the arrival of your newborn*. HealthyChildren.org. https://www.healthychildren.org/English/ages-stages/prenatal/delivery-beyond/Pages/Bringing-Baby-Home.aspx

Steen, M. (2023, June 18). *Why dads and their babies need to go skin-to-skin*. Scientific American. https://www.scientificamerican.com/article/why-dads-and-their-babies-need-to-go-skin-to-skin1/

Taylor, K. K. (2019, May 2). *Price Check: Are cloth diapers worth it? Or are they a bum deal?* Squawkfox. https://www.squawkfox.com/cloth-diapers/

Taylor, M. (2022, May 24). *The state of moms and dads in America*. Fatherhood. https://www.fatherhood.org/championing-fatherhood/the-state-of-moms-and-dads-in-america-2022

Tedesco, H., Weaver, J., & McCarthy, C. (2023, September 13). *4 ways to help your child adapt to life's rapid changes*. TIME. https://time.com/6313254/children-ai-life-changes-essay/

Tips for keeping your relationship alive after having your first baby. (n.d.). emmasdiary. https://www.emmasdiary.co.uk/pregnancy-and-birth/postnatal-wellbeing/tips-for-keeping-your-relationship-alive-after-having-your-first-baby

Toddler development and milestones. (2023). Michigan.gov. https://www.michigan.gov/mikidsmatter/parents/toddler/milestones#:

Winston, R., & Chicot, R. (2016). The importance of early bonding on the long-term mental health and resilience of children. *London Journal of Primary Care, 8*(1), 12–14. https://doi.org/10.1080/17571472.2015.1133012

Zauderer, S. (2023, July 21). *Diaper facts & statistics: Average cost of a diaper*. Cross River Therapy. https://www.crossrivertherapy.com/research/diaper-facts-statistics#:

IMAGE REFERENCES

Blum, B. (2018, August 5). *Toddlers at home* [Image]. In Unsplash. https://unsplash.com/s/photos/toddlers-at-home

Brankin62. (2012, January 4). *Family father beach child* [Image]. In Pixabay. https://pixabay.com/photos/family-father-beach-child-walking-11883/

Donnalynn52. (2020, February 27). *Dad new dad fathers day baby* [Image]. In Pixabay. https://pixabay.com/photos/dad-new-dad-fathers-day-baby-4885665/

Fields, R. (2017, August 2). *Boy playing cube on white wooden blocks* [Image]. In Pixabay. https://unsplash.com/photos/boy-playing-cube-on-white-wooden-table-Xz7MMD5tZwA

Jump1987. (2023, April 1). *Father dad baby girl* [Image]. In Pixabay. https://pixabay.com/photos/father-dad-baby-girl-love-kid-7855712/

Khaleel, W. (2019, April 7). *Baby's white and green diaper* [Image]. In Unsplashed. https://unsplash.com/photos/babys-white-and-green-diaper-pgSy1-dZkuw

Luenen, M. (2020, July 8). *Infant hand child father* [Image]. In Pixabay. https://pixabay.com/photos/infant-hand-child-father-parents-5385198/

947051. (2015, September 10). *Swimming pool pusinka family dad* [Image]. In Pixabay. https://pixabay.com/photos/swimming-pool-pusinka-family-dad-917604/

Public Domain Pictures. (2012, February 26). *Baby caucasian child dad daughter* [Image]. In Pixabay. https://pixabay.com/photos/baby-caucasian-child-dad-daughter-17316/

Tungart 7. (2024, February 16). *Grandparents-grandson-family-boy* [Image]. In Pixabay. https://pixabay.com/illustrations/grandparents-grandson-family-boy-8577355/

Sudakow, J. (2021, August 27). *4 Ways working dads can make more time for family*. Harvard Business Review. https://hbr.org/2019/04/4-ways-working-dads-can-make-more-time-for-family